Railroads and the Character of America, 1820–1887

Railroads and the
Character of America
1820-1887

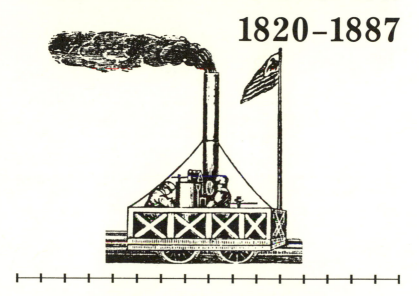

JAMES A. WARD

THE UNIVERSITY OF TENNESSEE PRESS : KNOXVILLE

Publication of this book has been aided by a grant from the American Council of Learned Societies from funds provided by the Andrew W. Mellon Foundation.

Grateful acknowledgment is made to the following:

Business History Review for permission to reprint portions of James A. Ward, "The Railway Corporate-State Metaphor: Image and Reality," Winter 1981, 491–516.

Railroad History for permission to reprint portions of James A. Ward, "On Time: Railroads and the Tempo of American Life," Autumn 1984, 87–95.

Line art courtesy of Historical Pictures Service, Inc., Chicago.

The paper used in this book meets the minimum requirements of the American National Standard for Permanence of Paper for Printed Library Materials, Z39.48-1984. Binding materials have been chosen for durability.

Library of Congress Cataloging-in-Publication Data

Ward, James Arthur, 1941–
   Railroads and the character of America, 1820–1887.

   Bibliography: p.
   Includes index.
   1. Railroads — United States — History — 19th century.
2. National characteristics, American. I. Title.
HE2751.W23 1986   385'.0973   85-22658
ISBN 0-87049-498-8 (alk. paper)

TO ANNE ELIZABETH,

Who, when she was eleven years old
Poignantly asked her father,
Who was as usual engrossed with what follows,
"Where are you, Daddy, when you are not here with us?"
This is a token repayment
For sometimes not being there.

CONTENTS

ILLUSTRATIONS

├──┼──┼──┼──┼──┼──┼──┼──┼──┼──┼──┼──┼──┼──┼──┼──┤

ACKNOWLEDGMENTS

An author has the opportunity to meet library and archives people who are among the nicest anywhere; they are surely the unsung heroes and heroines of the scholarly world. To thank all those who aided me in this would fill pages and risk leaving someone out. Instead I will just say thanks to them all from the Library of Congress and the Pennsylvania State Library to the busy staff at the Erwin Library in Boonville, New York. A special nod, however, must go to Neal Coulter, reference librarian at the University of Tennessee at Chattanooga, who is one of the most helpful in the business. He has an incredible ability (and willingness) to locate information, and he relishes the challenge.

Money is always important when writing a book, and I would be remiss if I did not thank the UTC Faculty Research Committee and the University of Chattanooga Foundation for two timely grants and the American Philosophical Society for its faith and investment in this project. Their financial aid helped me to defray travel and manuscript preparation costs. While still on the subject of money, I also wish to thank John Trimpey, dean of the Arts and Sciences at UTC, for granting me a Sabbatical that allowed the necessary time off from my teaching duties to finish this up. My typist, Elke Lawson, who labored cheerfully through two full drafts of the manuscript, already knows that she has my undying gratitude. Carol Orr, Director of the University of Tennessee Press, offered encouragement when I most needed it and, in her inimitable manner, cajoled a better book out of me. I cannot thank her enough.

Several people read parts or all of this and made helpful suggestions. Two anonymous referees for the *Business History Review* forced me to critically examine my methodology and greatly improved the chapter "The Problems of Empire" before it appeared in that journal in the winter of 1981. I want to thank them for their advice and the *Review*'s editor for allowing the article to be reproduced here. Robert Post, *Railroad History* editor, helped me to tighten up the chapter "On Time" that appeared in number 151 of his journal in the fall of 1984. I thank him for his efforts and for permission to reprint the article. James Oliver Robertson, whose *American Myth, American Reality* influenced many of my ideas in what follows, reviewed the manuscript and offered many suggestions for improvement; I took them all and appreciated every one.

Two close friends deserve special mention. H. Larry Ingle, with whom I once wrote a textbook, took time off from finishing up his book on the Quaker-Hicksite split to read every word herein; I am sure readers will appreciate the revisions he demanded I make. He is a rare colleague. My wife, Roberta Shannon Ward, also endured every word of this in several versions, pointed out many of its manifold weaknesses, and more importantly offered specific suggestions for improvement. For her unflagging encouragement and other more important things, all I can say here is many thanks.

JAMES A. WARD
Chattanooga, Tennessee
December 12, 1985

Railroads and the Character of America, 1820–1887

Upon Reflection

┣━┼━┼━┼━┼━┼━┼━┼━┼━┼━┼━┼━┼━┼━┼━┫

T HE character of America is an ambiguous and elusive concept. It is difficult to define, hard to document, and impossible to demonstrate. Yet it remains a beguiling challenge because many historians, I think, agree that there is a distinctive aura that envelopes the United States and its people. Americans look at the world differently, enjoy a unique historical perspective, and sometimes act in ways that seem peculiar to foreign eyes. That is about as far as the consensus on the character of the nation extends; the sources and contours of those peculiarities remain the subject for heated debates within the historical fraternity.

Several thoughtful authors have entered the fray and examined from various perspectives the question of what constitutes the character of America. Michael Kammen in his *People of Paradox* sought its origins in the country's deeply religious colonial past and then analyzed the paradoxes that developed in light of these beginnings. James Oliver Robertson investigated *American Myth, American Reality* to explain how Americans maintained their cherished dreams and expectations in spite of the tensions created by contradictory realities. Rush Welter looked into *The Mind of America* through the nation's Fourth of July orations to find its fears and aspirations. David Potter, on the other hand, convincingly argued that Americans are what they are because they are preeminently a *People of Plenty*. Economist John Kenneth Galbraith broadly agreed with that idea when he stamped the United States *The Affluent Society*. More recently Christopher Lasch took the 1970s, a period he characterized as "An Age of Diminishing Expectations," and pronounced the onset of *The Culture of Narcissism*. Others, most notably Frederick Jackson Turner, looked to the West for the American character's seedbed or to the permutations among Old World ideas and culture and the harsh realities of the New World's environment.[1]

The possibilities for an examination of the American character are endless. For the purposes of this volume, I am less interested in learning what motivates individual Americans than in determining what Americans of a certain era thought their nation was and, equally important, where they thought it was going. The character of any nation forms the bond that holds its people together in some measure of political and cultural harmony, and I am especially interested in uncovering shared assumptions, often unconsciously held, that linked Americans together during periods of profound change. To make the subject more workable, I have limited the breadth of my inquiry to roughly a sixty-year period in the middle of the nineteenth century. This selection is particularly poignant because sometime during that period the bonds loosened and finally gave way in a brutal civil war. By examining the ambitions, insecurities, hopes, and fears among certain promotional writers, I have tried to determine what common vision prompted them to a particular course of action — in this case the risking of the nation's surplus capital in an untried railroad technology.

I must confess that I did not set out to write this book. Instead, I was working on a volume tentatively entitled "Self-Made Worlds," in which I was interested to find out how men connected with the railroad industry viewed their business and its place in the larger society. More specifically, I was looking at their metaphorical expressions and the images that underlaid them for clues on how they perceived themselves. The railroad writers did not tell me that though; whether they lived in Maine or Texas, in slave or free societies, they persisted almost until the Civil War in writing more generally about how railways were perfectly in accord with the national character and were providentially sent to enable Americans to realize their grandest dreams. In the process railroad people, perhaps unwittingly, told us more about the broader context of their society than they did about their own business.

Upon reflection, this made sense to me. For the first thirty years of the railway age the industry was too young to have developed its own peculiar image and metaphors. That came only later. The early railroad promoters, engineers, and managers took on the coloration of the society around them and in turn reflected its character. In so doing, the writers displayed, at quite another level, their views and apprehensions about America's current conditions and their fears for its future. Because railroads were popular, they evoked a massive amount of literature, much of which looked into the future to see what the wonderful new age with rails would bring. Since the promoters were striving to convince fellow citizens that the rails were the nation's salvation, not to mention urging their contemporaries to open their purses liberally to finance construction, such advocates sought to strike common chords, to base their appeals upon shared national characteristics. The rapidity with which rails expanded across the eastern half of the United States in their first three decades testifies to the promoters' ability to identify and appeal to the main elements of the country's collective personality.

Very often railway writers' arguments were most compelling because of the language they chose rather than for any specific points they made. They skillfully selected metaphors that drew upon the common image Americans held of their nation's character. A quarter of a century ago Kenneth Boulding noted that we all create such images or mental representations of things perceived and then act upon them. The images are altered by incoming messages from the outside, and it is this slow evolutionary process of adding and creating mutant images that shapes our view of the world, Boulding contended, resulting in a congenial overall image that becomes more important to us than factual reality. The larger view creates and defines a metaphoric reality for us; what we think to be true, even about our own character, is more important than what is actually true.[2] Railroad advocates as early as the 1820s instinctively understood this notion and drew upon it to plead their case, arguing that railroads were perfectly in tune with the nation's existing character and would be instrumental in bettering it.

James Oliver Robertson later extended Boulding's ideas when he pointed out that the "juxtaposition of images and metaphors and ideals make[s] logic out of the rationally illogical." All elements of the national character did not have to be complementary, he reminded us, because physical reality and the life of the mind are untidy elements often working at cross-purposes. But one of the important functions of an overarching image, such as that of the national character, is to enable people to make sense of their complex, ever-changing worlds. Although such an image is intrinsically the sum of individual notions, Boulding explained, it promotes, if recognized widely enough, the acceptance of common values and outlooks. Furthermore, when the larger society accords any group's image its respect, then that group's vision becomes "an image of the society itself." Thus, prominent leaders, such as railway promoters and executives, sought to define and shape the larger society to conform to their business's image. Their widely read literature agreed upon certain basic presuppositions about the national character that served both to reinforce the prevailing image and at the same time to alter it. As Boulding said, our actions are predicated upon how we perceive ourselves within the larger image and "our behaviour depends upon the image."[3]

Any image, especially one as nebulous as a national character, is revealed most dramatically in a society's metaphors and analogies. Bruce Mazlish, in one of the more singular railroad books to appear in years, *The Railroad and the Space Program*, explained that "one reason for this is that analogies or metaphors establish a relationship, often emotional as well as logical, between otherwise disparate items." Michel Foucault, in his search for the basis of knowledge, located that relationship in "a network of analogies that transcend the traditional proximities." Robertson concurred, tying myths to images to metaphors with the observation that:

> . . . myths bundle together images and symbols, metaphors and models, and complex ideas. . . . [and] in modern American society provide available images by which we, perhaps unconsciously but nevertheless consistently and continuously, attempt to resolve the contradictions and paradoxes in our lives, measure the world we live in, judge it, explain it to ourselves and others, define our reality and act upon it.

In a more literary vein, Leo Marx in his *The Machine in the Garden* avers that when a writer uses a metaphor "he seizes upon the symbolic property or meaning in the event itself — its capacity to express much of what he thinks and feels about his situation" to explain how his private situation corresponds with his image of the larger character of his society.[4]

Railway writers' images, mirrored in their metaphors, exposed a profound uneasiness about America, fears they correctly assumed millions of their fellow citizens shared. Rail advocates thought it only made sense, for example, to promote their projects on the basis that they would secure the nation's defense, because many of their readers thought that the United States was militarily weak. The same kinds of assumptions gave rise to their claims that railways would cure poverty, ignorance, and poor health. The sheer volume of literature dealing with land values, perhaps aimed at poor rural constituents, the "country" political factions, and their promises to unlock western treasures, says volumes about rural conditions and western myths and realities. Promoters continually stressed the need to act quickly in order to outstrip various dangers they feared could overtake the nation. This emphasis on haste must have proved a powerful inducement to investors; similar entreaties were made for decades in all sections and out west long after the war. Whether the promoters' fears were justified was less important than the fact that enthusiasts were convinced they were real enough and appealed for public support on that basis. If there was one theme that pervaded all the literature, it was that the nation had to change — and quickly. To stand still, promoters claimed, would be fatal.

For insight into how railroads reflected the American character, I sought out public railway materials whenever possible. I had no other options, largely because very few company records survived from the early period. Those that did were primarily engineering reports and construction correspondence that tended to be very narrowly focused. Instead, I examined railroad items taken from newspapers, government committee reports, the few articles of railroad interest that appeared in literary magazines, railroad annual reports, and reporters' descriptions of large public gatherings that endorsed rail construction. The *American Railroad Journal*, founded in 1832, was most helpful. Its two editors, D. Kimball Minor (until February 1849) and Henry Varnum Poor, exchanged copies of their paper with other editors around the country; Minor and Poor then reprinted in their *Journal* articles of railway interest they found in their incoming mail. This tradition, common among newspapermen, enabled the New Yorkers to keep up with railroad news all over the land. Surprisingly the *Journal* published a great deal of information gleaned from southern and midwestern papers. While such selection was at best random, over almost forty years any sectional inequalities in the number of published articles pretty well balanced out. Hezekiah Niles's *Weekly Register* was also helpful, though Niles, a prominent border-state Whig, had interests that ranged far beyond railroads. Nevertheless, he was a strong supporter of internal improvements and, like any talented editor, it was his wont occasionally to take the larger view to generalize about how the rails harmonized with the basic nature of his country.

Railway writers, it is important to note, were predominantly men who were instrumental in creating favorable public opinion to support continued construction. Few were on the inside of the rail business; the hectic nature of the infant industry seldom allowed railroad managers the leisure to reflect on how their company illustrated the larger character of America. Those who molded the public's attitudes, however, were certainly no less important to the rails' success. Legislators on important internal improvement committees that drafted laws and public pronouncements, editors everywhere but especially near the nation's financial districts, civil engineers who put together colorful pamphlets praising their lines' locations and predicting myriad benefits from their construction, and even poets, essayists, and book reviewers were the people who created and popularized the images and metaphors that linked the industry with the larger national character. They were also the men who divined what America was all about. In their state houses, editorial offices, and merchants' exchanges, they were important people, literate, certainly persuasive, frequently well-to-do, and often politically active, who shaped opinions. They interpreted a new, sometimes frightening, and often unintelligible technology in terms of their image of the larger nation.

These men, whom I label promoters, enthusiasts, and advocates, were among the most important to the railroad business in its first thirty years, and they provide the grist for the first part of this book. After its small-scale beginnings in the late 1840s, the public railway literature began to change perceptibly; it became more concerned with private than public welfare. Enthusiasts started to promote their projects on the basis that rail enterprises would be profit-making ventures rather than that they would cure the ills that racked the nation. By the following decade the industry had plainly begun to take on a life of its own. Writers both inside and out became more interested in management structures, accounting principles, securities markets, technological innovations, and operating procedures than in the general weal. Expert managers became more important to the business than the editors and writers who generalized about its place in the larger society.

Thus, the sources for this book necessarily shift in its later parts. Annual reports, business letters, and newspaper accounts of railroad leaders' activities supplant the older promotional pieces. In many respects these materials were more difficult to deal with in light of the book's approach, as these writers were less reflective than the earlier generation and less given to grand pronouncements and theoretical forays into the future. They were a more close-mouthed set of men, and unfortunately much of their correspondence either has not survived or is locked away and probably forgotten in corporate warehouses. Although railway officials may have been more insulated from public attitudes, their language, metaphors, and actions illustrated that they, too, operated under strong presumptions about the character of their nation. Their view of the national character was very different from that of their predecessors, but, like them, later railway promoters were in positions to help alter aspects of that character.

The book's dichotomy makes the shifts in the railroad industry's views of the nation's character appear more well defined than they actually were. When images and metaphors change it is often in a sporadic and uneven process. Some promoters, for example, began to modify their views of the nation soon after the 1839 depression hit, but it took over a decade for their notions to become widely held. Moreover, the farther one traveled west from the Atlantic Coast the less the changes were evident. Those areas where rails were still being introduced retained the 1830s' images much longer than did their more economically mature eastern counterparts. Some of the geographical differences reflected peculiar sectional characteristics, but looking at them from the viewpoint of the railroad industry they were also a function of the degree of transport maturity. The image of the railroad as a promoter of national unity still lived in parts of the West as late as the 1870s, long after it had been laid to rest in Massachusetts, New York, and Georgia. Such ideas flowed across the country like tides from the Northeast into the South and West, and the images that eventually captured Americans' imaginations in the interior were usually those easterners had adopted a decade or more earlier. They spread slowly, and the language that reflected them did even more so. To make sense of this uneven flow, I have used eastern images as a bench mark for making chronological divisions.

Many people will recognize this book's end date, 1887, as the year the Interstate Commerce Act was passed. Aimed specifically at railroads, the bill that established the Interstate Commerce Commission was less the abrupt end of an era than the beginning of the end of a distinct period that had begun before the Civil War. Americans' perceptions of their polity were again changing. The whole notion that relatively unfettered competition was good for everybody was on the wane and would later bring increased bureaucratization to everyone's life. The ICC was just the start, but it stood out as such a landmark piece of legislation in American political annals that I have used it here more for its symbolic value than for any other reason.

Because the topic is so large, the time period so long, and the changes so chronologically erratic, the book is not a traditional history in the sense that it explains causes and chronicles changes over time. Instead, it is more a series of essays, each examining a broad spectrum of railway literature on a topic that illustrates prominent aspects of the character of America. None of them is meant to be a history of railroad development or American thought. Rather than proceeding along a horizontal time continuum, the book identifies two important overall themes and discusses them in some depth. This is not an intellectual odyssey through Americans' minds during the period; it contains aspects of intellectual history in that I have proceeded from the premise that ideas, and the images that overlaid them, were as important as any perceived realities. The book melds aspects of literary criticism with the more traditional historian's task of textual analysis to reexamine the literature of a business group that dominated the nation's consciousness before the Civil War and the country's affairs shortly afterward.

Railroad leaders were such successful promoters and managers and they amassed so much political, social, and economic influence that their assumptions about the character of their nation became important. In many Americans' minds the industry became a vital metaphor representing the nation's hopes and aspirations. Rail advocates and executives therefore were in a position to help redefine America's character. In so doing they gave Americans a clearer sense of who they were and what they were becoming.

CHAPTER 1

The Metaphors of Fear and Hope

⊢——┼——┼——┼——┼——┼——┼——┼——┼——┼——┼——┼——┼——┼——┤

AMERICANS had deeply ambivalent images of their nation's character in the second quarter of the nineteenth century. Railway promoters' metaphors displayed an inordinate pride in the country's success but at the same time exhibited manifold doubts about its future. Because railroad spokesmen were trying to sell their fellow countrymen on the benefits expected from the introduction of railways, they naturally focused on views of a better future rather than upon their specific fears. Americans had reason to worry, however. Barely a decade removed from an indecisive war with Great Britain, they had just endured their first great political convulsion over slavery in the 1820 Missouri Compromise debates, had felt threatened by John C. Calhoun's attempt to redefine the Constitution, and had sadly watched the first generation of revolutionary figures pass away.

Their new political leaders gave Americans further pause with some of their observations. Henry Clay, not exactly a man given to public self-doubts and fears, wrote in 1833 that "we have no past, no future. After forty-five years of existence under the present Constitution, what single principle is fixed?" If that question issued from a man who epitomized western enthusiasm, witness John Quincy Adams, a man always disposed to look on the bleak side, who noted in his memoirs: "one-third of the people is perverted, one-third slumbers, and the rest wring their hands with unavailing lamentations in the foresight of evil which they cannot avert." The Frenchman, Alexis de Tocqueville, lent a foreign perspective to Americans' self-doubts when he pronounced: "I shall refuse to believe in the duration of a government that is called upon to hold together forty different nations spread over a territory equal to one half of Europe." Those Americans who resented foreign doomsayers could look to their own Calhoun who warned his countrymen that "the very idea of an *American People*, as constituting a single community, is mere chimera."[1]

Numerous Americans counterbalanced such misgivings by enthusiastically promoting railways as the country's best hope for achieving a much desired national unity. Their zeal for railroads was pervasive and contagious. When the Chevalier de Gerstner visited the United States in 1837 he was amazed at Americans' enthusiasm for railways. He reported that no sooner had he stepped on board his ship in Liverpool than

> the first American paper that caught his eye was the *"Railroad Journal."* During his sickness, which lasted through the voyage he says, he remembers of the conversation on board only the word *"Railroad."* When he arrived in New-York he was shown among other things, a *"Marine Railroad,"* for hauling up ships for repair. In the lead mines of Pennsylvania he saw a *"Railroad"* under ground. At a Southern manufactory of a very extensive character, one of the chief curiosities was a *"Railroad suspended in the air."* . . . When he visited one of the *prisons*, in Philadelphia, we believe, after having gone the rounds, the overseer exclaimed, but you have not seen my *"Railroad."*[2]

The statistics reinforced his observations. Armed with the powerful promise of national unity, the promoters, who labored hard and long in the railways' behalf starting in the 1820s, prevailed, and the physical manifestations of their efforts were soon everywhere. By 1837 railroad companies in the United States operated 1,498 miles of road and at the next census had completed an additional 1,330 miles despite the 1837 panic and the tightening grip of the depression that began two years later. The mania was unrelenting: by the end of the 1840s the "iron horse" meandered over 8,021 miles of rails, a figure destined to triple in the following decade.[3]

Implicit in all these numbers were thousands of new jobs and a rising demand for a variety of new skills required to operate roads reliably and safely. Lumber, coal, glass, iron, construction, and lubrication businesses located anywhere near the new lines prospered in their wake. Bankers, brokers, printers, newspaper editors, whalers, even sandwich-makers, cashed in on the new riches. Railways equally benefitted shippers, importers and exporters, manufacturers, miners, farmers, and almost every other occupational group imaginable. As Douglas T. Miller has observed, culturally, politically, economically, socially, and in every other manner this was *The Birth of Modern America.*[4] Moreover, in that second quarter of the century the rails helped to bring seven new states into the union, although even their most rabid supporters could not claim credit for California. If the Chevalier was any true indicator of public opinion, the nation was railway mad.

The rails' unprecedented popularity was in large measure due to the promoters' skills in appealing to Americans' deepest fears about the character of their national experiment. They hammered again and again at their theme that the iron roads would forever unite the country. Their readers, at least on the conscious level, must have come to expect such a sermon in any piece of railroad material. The enthusiasts' judicious choice of metaphors, however, indicated that the topic also had a powerful subconscious appeal. In fact, they adeptly promoted their projects on both strata; railways, they claimed, would provide a highly visible national prosperity and mobility while also effecting closer, friendlier relations on the personal, state, and regional levels. More subtly, rail advocates' images and metaphors also promised a moral, intellectual, class, and most of all political intimacy that many Americans feared could not be achieved through any other means.

Early railroad enthusiasts always strove to promote their projects as national in character and destined to improve the common weal. They played down any notion that their roads were designed to encourage one city or region at the expense of another. Indeed some, like the 1831 Pennsylvania Legislative Internal Improvements Committee, recommended that state tax revenues be used in part to help other states build improvements because, as the committee boldly proclaimed, "the policy of Pennsylvania has been to consider all states of the union as dependent on each other, and bound together much more by commerce among the several states, than by any force of written constitution."[5] Even by that early date Americans were convinced that railways could make the United States smaller, more compact and intimate even as they pushed it outward to extend and open the continent's vast interior. Enthusiasts chose to believe that railroads could be both centrifugal and centripetal simultaneously, an inherent paradox if ever there were one.

The paradox, however, explains why the idea of railroads so quickly took the country by storm. The new form of transport could unite discordant existing images; railways could at the same time serve individual betterment and the public good. By spending public monies freely, the nation could promote sturdier individualism. Ideas would travel as far and fast as merchandise. Abstractions and prosperity would make Americans freer and prosperous men have no reason to quarrel. The private image served the public and railways served them both; railroads encouraged the nation's heartfelt hopes and aspirations while quelling its very deepest fears.

In the first two decades of the railway age therefore, its advocates exhausted their repertoire of national unity images and metaphors, always emphasizing their mutually beneficial rather than predatory aspect. They studiously avoided the idea that one entity might wax fat at the expense of another and made no allusions to the rapid growth of a wealthy class, of one or two prominent cities, or of one section of the country. They much preferred to extrapolate from a local improvement the good and welfare of the whole. And no matter how insignificant or small the railroad project, a talented promoter could with slight exertion blow it metaphorically out of proportion to serve the national unity image. Any railway over ten miles long that harbored the slightest predisposition to purchase a steam locomotive was, to read its enthusiasts, dutifully engaged in tying the West or the South or Someplace securely to the nation for the greater glory of all.

Promoters positively blanched at any mention that their projects might be weapons designed for use in urban commercial wars. That whole notion smacked of an unwelcome divisiveness, and they were

sure the nation already had a surplus of that. The idea that railroads could be offensive and defensive instruments was a development of the 1850s, a decade brimming with conflicts. That first
generation of railroad promoters was another breed entirely, and
how it viewed itself may be judged from the fact that it invited John
Carroll of Carrollton, the last surviving signer of the Declaration
of Independence, to break ground for the nation's first railway in
1828. Clearly the B&O's promoters, like those that followed them,
looked far above petty local issues and felt that in building a railroad they were doing their patriotic duty to bind their country together. Of course they often paid lip service to the needs of their
nearby port cities, but the vast majority, judging from their literature, really believed that their railroads would bring increased prosperity to all. There would be no winners or losers. Advocates sometimes even wholeheartedly supported projects designed to *increase*
a nearby city's trade. That early generation of promoters preferred
to argue that while cities' populations, real estate values, and regis-
tered shipping tonnages might change, their relative positions, at
least among those wise enough to invest in the railway future, would
remain the same; everyone in them would enjoy elevated living standards and opportunities.

In support of that notion many writers pointed out that cities
all had captive trade territories that nobody else's improvement could
capture. Instead, they argued, the new railroads were really only
competing for the very distant markets, the developing ones that
lacked secure eastern trade alliances. A writer for the Baltimore
Patriot combined these two ideas in 1835 when he reported that
Philadelphia "now enjoys the benefit of direct communication with
western waters, and these two great cities [Philadelphia and Balti-
more] are now engaged in successful competition for the trade of
the western country." In that writer's view both were succeeding.
When D. Kimball Minor, founder of the *American Railroad Journal* up in New York City, thought about it eight years later, however, he decided such competitive successes had to be defined in
even larger terms. The editor resorted to a homely metaphor, saying "thus have *Baltimore, Philadelphia,* and *Boston* shaken hands
with the *people* in all directions, invited them to *dinner* and treated
them to the delicacies of their extensive markets — who will of course

reciprocate their civilities and send them milk, butter, eggs, and bacon in return." Everyone, urban, rural, easterner and westerner, feasted at Minor's metaphorical banquet, all brought together to enjoy the wholesome products of the West made possible by the railroad.[6]

Railway writers, like Minor, in those first decades of railway enthusiasm never tired of conjuring up such comforting metaphors. Their considerable ingenuity in devising such illustrations gives much of the period's literature its color and interest. They likened railways to almost any commonplace thing that came to mind: the human body and its various parts; the family with its tightly knit constituents; adolescence with its joys and impetuosity; trees, trunks, and branches; water in its various states, rivers, floods, streams, tides, and rain, thereby distilling every possible symbolism from that simple liquid; iron bands, hoops, loops, and various other iron ties. In keeping with most people's interests, writers kept their metaphors rural, taking their themes from nature, and strove always for simplicity. Metaphors are supposed to take something uncommon, complicated, and sometimes frightening, and make it familiar, intelligible, and friendly. Promoters in those early years certainly succeeded.

If the metaphors had anything in common, it was that they drew together, linked, joined, or somehow interconnected various parts, in a linguistic transmutation of the railroads' actual functions. By implication, the metaphors provided some sharp insights into what Americans perceived to be the character of their nation. That an overwhelming majority of the metaphors at least touch upon the promise that rails will finally unite the nation says much about Americans' uncertainty about their future. And many of the metaphorical expressions display a nervous edge; they are a little too enthusiastic and too effusive, even allowing for their promotional intent. They reveal a deep fear that the nation will not endure, much less prevail. Many of the metaphors radiate an almost desperate energy, an intimation that railways might be the last hope for holding the political experiment together. Plainly worried about intensifying sectional feelings, promotional writers emphasized the common interests that bound Americans together. Many seemed certain that railroads were a safe, neutral enthusiasm that could transcend the bitter problems for which there appeared no solutions. Their metaphors, if only because they were too often overblown in their insistence on the unifying powers of the railroad, reveal an uneasiness about the future prospects of their young nation.

One of the earliest popular metaphorical constructs to illustrate the notion of interconnection was the likening of the railroad's place in society to the functioning of the human body. Dr. Charles Caldwell, a Boston physician, was professionally attracted to this theme and gave one of the best expositions of it while speaking at a meeting in Lexington in 1831. The very title of his address that evening was a tipoff, "On the Moral and Other Indirect Influences of Railroads." In a strikingly modern tone Caldwell argued for "a federalized system of Rail-roads" connecting each state to the nation's capital. "I mean by it," he explained, "a system analogous to that of the blood vessels of the human body, where minor ramifications, running from the remote parts, connect themselves with others, in their course, and unite in main ones, to empty their contents in the cavity of the heart." Presumably Washington, D.C. was the metaphorical equivalent of the "cavity of the heart."[7]

It did not take a physician to see the metaphorical resemblance between railroads and human circulation; other observers also picked it up. Compilers of corporate annual reports are usually a bland lot, but the author of the 1840 edition of the Louisville, Cincinnati & Charleston Railroad's yearly effort showed the staying power of the idea. Railroads, he opined, "like the veins and arteries of the human . . . are in the physical and commercial world but parts of one system, the circulation of the one, depended on, and contributing to the circulation of all." Railways did not simply conjure up blood images; other bodily parts and functions also seemed appropriately analogous. An anonymous letter-writer, arguing that the first decade's railroads were shoddily built when they should instead have been created for posterity, couched his appeal in a combination of patriotic and metaphorical terms that he knew would strike a sympathetic chord, "now that the beginning has been made, and the gristle of our young republic is hardening into bone, and its thews and sinews are becoming strong and matured, let us do" he called, "worthy of our resources, our native talent, our destiny." Others of a more scatalogical bent plumbed the depths of this metaphor. In an unsigned 1845 editorial, "The Farmers and The Railroads," the *American Railroad Journal* writer pictured an integrated transport system: "The steamboat skirts the shore to landings whence roads lead into the interior. The railroad plunges at once into the bowels of the land and drains the produce from either side like a mighty river and its tributaries."[8] Underlying that ghastly metaphorical image was a more fundamental agrarian view of life. In the promotional period of railroad development, the industrial influence sometimes seeped into the bodily metaphors, although with somewhat less vivid results. In a toast delivered at the opening ceremonies of the Harlem Railroad in 1839 a William Paxton Hallart offered: "*The Empire State* — Interlaced with veins of iron, who shall put a limit to the development of her gigantic resources?" The next glass raiser, a John Greenfield, carried the metaphor one step farther when he boomed out to the assembled crowd: "*The United States* — Linked together, not only by ties of friendship, but by bands of iron — May both ties and bands be equally indissoluble." Presumably the bands of iron referred back to the first speaker's metal veins as well as to the ties of friendship. In any event these were rather grand sentiments to be inspired by a road that did not even reach the Westchester County line.

As demonstrated by the toasts at the Harlem's grand opening, the imagery of various bodily parts and functions, all bound together by the forged bands of railroad iron, slipped easily into the corollary metaphor of the family, the unity of blood kin drawn together by the same ties. Joseph Bloomfield, the third to the podium, made this transition with ease. To "*Railroads,*" he proposed, "the great desideratum — to bind the Union in an iron band of brothers. An improvement of the age, as important and necessary to connect all parts of the Union with their commercial centre, New York." The various metaphorical specifics were often at variance; Bloomfield's "centre" of the nation was located a couple of hundred miles north of Dr. Caldwell's "cavity." At the risk of repeating all the toasts raised at the opening of an insignificant railroad, although that occasion must have been a veritable metaphorical feast, we must record one more. The next luminary to hold forth, Isaac Gibson, soared to new heights: "*Railroads throughout the world,*" he intoned, "they have brought the great family of mankind into nearer and more

The South Carolina Railroad hired a band
to help celebrate a locomotive's maiden run.
(Brown, *The History of the First Locomotives in America*)

genial communion — they have levelled old prejudices — created new affinities — and given new impetus to the great cause of civilization. May their extent be unlimited."[9]

At a similar occasion eight years later Minor returned to the same theme, only he had a more sharply limited geographical area in mind. In a lengthy editorial on what a railroad system meant for the nation, he declared, "we cannot but view the introduction of the system as the means — greater than any, we may say than *all* other — of perpetuating our glorious union. It will prove literally, . . . as bands of iron binding us together, a family of states — thus ensuring our greatness and permanence as a nation." Toasts seemed to have brought out the more expansive family metaphors, as for example at a Pittsburgh St. Patrick's Day celebration in 1837 when someone stood up and used railroads as a metaphor for progress. "Education," he announced, was "the great Railroad of *internal* improvement; may the main line and the branches be extended and continued, until it pervades all the ends of the earth, and brings the Nations as one Family, to the great Author and universal Centre of truth, liberty, peace and happiness."[10]

Having metaphorically coursed from capillaries through hearts to family ties and finally the brotherhood of man under God, all on iron rails, the promoters had pretty well exhausted their stock. A spellbinder at a railroad dinner in Natchez, Mississippi, however, made the transition nicely into an allied metaphorical image: the robust youthfulness of the new nation. He raised his toast to "*Internal Improvements* — The talisman whose magic influence will call into active exertions the giant energies of our youthful State; hers is the charm to make the wilderness glad, and the waste places to blossom as the rose." The new railroads were the magic that would hasten, in his case, Mississippi's maturity. Youth was more often used, however, as a metaphor for growth, as in a letter simply signed "X," sent to the *Railroad Journal.* In looking back over only nine years of railway building, "X" was astonished that hopes could "have been cherished of the rapidity with which it seems this country is destined to arrive at greatness unparalleled by any other nation whilst in a state of adolescence." To Minor, an indefatigable promoter of everything railroad, its development was proof itself of the adolescent nation's vitality. "There is nothing, perhaps, which more clearly demonstrates the immense resources of this young Republic," he argued, "and the energy of its inhabitants, than the boldness with which its facilities for internal communications are undertaken to be improved, and the rapidity with which they are completed when undertaken."[11]

Others were not so sure. The editor of the Savannah *Georgian*, usually a steady southern voice supporting internal improvements, sounded very discouraging when he picked up the youth metaphor in 1842. He ventured to think it might "be safely stated that our knowledge of the ultimate value of railroads, is, as yet, comparatively nothing. We see only the effect of infant energies and incipient efforts, and as we cannot tell what may be the mature developments, even of the most promising child, so, neither can we," he concluded, do it for railroads. His gloom was only matched by T.G. McCulloh, president of the Cumberland Valley Railroad, whose job it was to report to the Pennsylvania legislature in 1838 explaining why his railroad was so shoddily built. His was the plight of many other railroad officials; in a rather rare *mea culpa*, McCulloh explained that "our road was pushed on more rapidly than was perhaps prudent or judicious. The amount of stock subscribed was inadequate to the construction of a complete, permanent, and substantial road. It became then the great object to do the work on the most economical plan."[12]

The early promoters were consummate wordsmiths, likening railways to everything from trees to iron bands, but their metaphors tended to fall into two broad categories with regard to the theme of national unity: those metaphors that renewed, flowed, moved, and expanded and those that constricted, bound together, and held forever immobile. While on the surface they seem two quite distinct metaphorical categories, in fact they vividly illustrate the common overall image. For railroads did tie together irrevocably while moving outward at the same time. They were always moving in noisy, clattering, and dirty motion, but their superstructure, buildings, and permanent service structures were fixed, built to last, and often the most impressive structures in the towns and villages they served. Railways were paradoxical physical manifestations of motion, progress, and stasis, depending upon what aspect of their presence the promoters emphasized.

Even the language of the rails suggested metaphors. That railroads had trunk lines that connected with branch roads that served the outlying districts naturally gave rise to the tree metaphor. Moreover, trees, wood, and crosses have long served man as symbols for life and the family; family tree samplers were popular household staples in the period. Also, railways were introduced in an era of renewed religious fervor across the country as camp meetings, evangelists, and revivals drew large crowds everywhere. During such religious intensity some promoters must have been struck by the connection between Christ, who died on the tree-shaped cross with the promise of salvation for all enlightened mankind, and railroads which, supported and financed by the faithful, promised a form of salvation here on earth. Trees also symbolized the railroads' two principal physical attributes, they were stationary and rooted, yet within their vital fluids were in constant motion, bringing nourishment and growth to even the remotest part of their being.

Minor grasped the essential elements of the tree metaphor in an 1843 editorial on the proposal for a railroad from Hartford to Springfield. He decided the road would promote Boston's interests, because, he noted, "like the tree whose sap descends in the autumn through the trunk to the roots, and ascends again on the return of mild breezes in the spring to the branches, so will flow a vast amount of business to and from that enterprizing and calculating city." Minor was angry because his own city of New York was not part of that tree and therefore the commercial sap would benefit its more northerly rival. Like most promoters, Minor could also mix his metaphors; witness his later assertion that Boston "has labored at the *oar* and the *anvil* until she has spread herself all over the country."[13]

The tree metaphor suggested to some thoughtful promoters the idea of rain, the symbol of renewal and growth, most appropriate for the young republic. They ignored water's symbolic cleansing aspects to concentrate on its nourishing qualities and the fruits that would be realized from it. Minor, for example, excerpted the following thought from some report: "the great trade of the West — a trade, the future magnitude of which is so vast that we scarcely yet perceive the falling of the great drops which denote the overcharge of this cloud." A few months later the New York editor tried his own hand at a rainfall metaphor. Supporting plans building the

New York and Erie Railroad, he observed that it "will give new life and energy to the business operations of the State. It will prove . . . a refreshing and fertilizing shower which will unquestionably enable thousands to reap golden harvests."[14] A beautiful metaphor, well suited to the agrarian world, that promised timely sustenance and a future bonanza — exactly what railway enthusiasts had been promising all along.

Enough rain leads to the formation of lakes, oceans, and mighty rivers, and, indeed, several large bodies of water worked their way into railroad metaphors. Hezekiah Niles managed to use tides as a metaphor twice in the same article while discussing in 1839 the best way to travel from Charleston to New York. After mentioning several new southern roads, he confidently forecast in his *Register* that "a flood of travel will sweep via the route to Philadelphia in nearly a day less than by the other route." Later he described the wonders of the Portsmouth Railroad in Virginia predicting "the tide has set in its favor and it will go sweeping on till the whole travel of the south will pour in this direction." Floods reminded Minor of mighty rivers, drawing strength from their branches, always swelling. Discussing the importance of railroads drawing trade from the people located along their lines, he concluded "rivers increase in volume as they receive the successive tributaries which flow into them," and noted, "so with railroads between important points."[15]

J.D.B. De Bow in New Orleans, always enthusiastic about southern ventures into manufacturing and transportation, came up with an arresting metaphor that had one foot firmly planted in the camp of those who envisioned rails as always in motion and the other with those who saw them as a constricting force. De Bow was promoting what he called the Southern Atlantic and Mississippi Railroad; actually, he wanted a string of small roads built to fill the remaining gaps from Atlanta to the Mississippi River. If this became one continuous route, he declared "it would be another FATHER OF RIVERS, or rather an *iron stream*, intersecting and blessing a region almost as great in extent as that he blesses." It takes a powerful vision to elicit an image of an "iron stream," but if a great deal of license is allowed the metaphor actually makes some sense.[16]

The constriction metaphors were much more popular from the mid 1840s on, whereas motion imagery and the likening of railroads to natural phenomena had earlier been preferred. This change reflected the increased attention paid to political debates over the question of slavery. As the political rhetoric heated up, railway promoters reacted by drawing metaphors that were less diffuse, less aesthetically pleasing, and a great deal more firm. While political forces threatened to blow the country apart, railway advocates emphasized their own ability to bind it together. They became fascinated by iron and the powerful images that metal could evoke. Occasionally they still made some metaphorical reference to movement, but by the Mexican War that was clearly of secondary interest. They were looking for permanence.

They found the notion of iron bands to be a useful metaphor with its implication of the rails' potential for binding states indissolubly together. The Boston *Courier* in 1847 was one of the earliest to use this idea when its editor began a piece on New England railroads by observing "since Maine has been re-annexed to Massachusetts by the iron bonds of the Eastern and Maine railroads," the Bay State had accomplished through industrial means what she had not been able to do politically. That year another editor in Tennessee wrote in his Trenton *Emporium* that "these railroads are the iron bands that will bind the various sections of our beloved country together by a community of interest and fraternal feeling, and it is hoped, will render our union indissoluble." Henry Varnum Poor, Minor's successor to the *American Railroad Journal*'s editorial tasks, also loved the iron bondage theme. In a long article in which he examined the emerging systems growing out of the fragmented independent companies, he concluded that "with no other principle than the laws of trade and the local interest of the different sections, the Union is being fast bound together with these iron bands." Lest anyone miss his meaning, Poor explained, "all engaged in this work are co-laborers together for the good of the whole."

Poor also came up with an interesting variant to the iron bands metaphor, and one that was ahead of its time. When the roads unite, he said, "the iron rail will become another electric wire through which any persons upon a line of railway in the most remote part of the country can touch every section of the Union." Metaphorically the difference between iron bands and wires was minor, but Poor had neatly selected an image from another scientific advance and brought it into the railway world two years before the railroads first used a telegraph.[17]

Other iron metaphors differed in details but still evoked the same imagery. For example, John Roebling, later of Brooklyn Bridge fame, worried in 1847 that mid-Atlantic cities were not active enough in securing the inland urban trade. In a report he appealed to wealthy retired capitalists to unlock their strongboxes for the new Pennsylvania Central, warning "unless Rip wakes up and puts forth *arms of iron*, to clasp them to a closer embrace, they will soon become totally estranged from us, and derive their partial supplies from New Orleans, N. York and Boston." The editor of the Cincinnati *Gazette* came up with another variant when he wrote that "any one who will cast his eye over the map of central Indiana, will see that the State Capital is weaving a handsome little iron net about her, to make up for the absence of natural channels of trade." And Minor drew an image that was guaranteed to give his readers metaphorical claustrophobia; he managed to bind the railroads with their own rails. He was responding to a debate in the pages of his journal over whether railroads should be built to carry more than their expected trade. Minor said yes, arguing: "We must remember that the infant railroad is to be clothed in an iron suit, which can neither be altered or stretched,— if we give him a right fit at once, he can never grow any larger, and if we desire his future welfare, we must at first allow him some spare room." At least one railway advocate, the Rev. Dr. Flint, located his iron metaphor in the future. At the opening of the Eastern Railroad in Massachusetts in 1838, the Reverend toasted, "Railroads — the strong clamps which are destined to bind together with ribs of steel the whole of this great country; may they be multiplied and extended till they shall have cemented the Union beyond the possibility of severance."[18]

These were not the metaphors of parochial men; their common theme showed that early railroad enthusiasts shared an image of what their nation had to do to survive and prosper. They recognized the basic divisions that threatened the nation and were in fundamental agreement over the need for lasting internal ties, especially as the Union expanded geographically. Promoters bowed to local interests just enough to prompt citizens to invest their money in a largely untried technology, but those nods to urban and state rivalries were perfunctory at best and always couched in gentlemanly tones. They felt more comfortable using railroads, metaphorically and otherwise, to bring Americans together. The national unity image, revealed in their metaphors, was an expression of what rail advocates hoped the character of their nation would become, but it also implicitly exposed the major faults they saw in their national character. Railroad enthusiasts were unalloyed optimists, however, and they looked forward to the future, anticipating that they would change the very face of their nation. Their security in that belief rested on a prime assumption that the national character was also mercurial and volatile. They persistently referred to Americans as "a locomotive people" and counted on the truth of that metaphor to help effect a transformation of the national character.

CHAPTER 2

Taming the Iron Horse

├─┼─┼─┼─┼─┼─┼─┼─┼─┼─┼─┼─┼─┼─┼─┼─┤

IN the third decade of the nineteenth century Americans began to define their character in light of the new railroads. They liked the idea that it took a special race of people to foresee and capitalize on the promise of science. Promoters used the steam engine as a metaphor for what they thought Americans were and what they were becoming. They frequently discussed parallels between the locomotive and national character, pointing out that both possessed youth, power, speed, single-mindedness, and bright prospects. The metaphors, however, had their dark side. A locomotive was quite unlike anything Americans had ever seen. It was large, mysterious, and dangerous; many thought it a monster waiting to devour the unwary. Iron horse metaphors therefore served at least two purposes: they assuaged fears about inherent defects in the national character, prompting images of a more secure future, while they also made an alien technology less frightening, and even comforting and congenial.

Poor drew the important elements of the image together in 1851. "Look at the results of this material progress—" he wrote:

> the vigor, life and executive energy that follow in its train, rapidly succeeded by wealth, the refinement and intellectual culture of a high civilization. All this is typified, in a degree,

by a locomotive. The combination in its construction of nice art and the scientific application of a power our fathers knew not of, its speed surpassing that of the proudest courser in his untamed fleetness, and its immense strength, all are characteristic of our age and its tendencies. There was no need of a locomotive in former times. It would not have been in harmony with their modes of doing business or their habits of thought. To us, like the telegraph, it is essential, it constitutes a part of our nature, is a condition of our being what we are.[1]

Poor was, of course, promoting acceptance of railroads and enticing his readers to open their pocketbooks. But he was also defining the character of Americans by showing the locomotive to be a physical manifestation of their progressive tendencies.

The generation that identified itself with the locomotive, however, shared with its progenitors the queasy feeling that the railroads' bright expectations might not be realized. And the old fear of Americans' self-destructive tendencies appeared in the locomotive literature, as Poor illustrated when he declared that locomotives (or railroads or other technological improvements of the age, his antecedent is unclear) "are to become the necessities of every land, harmonizing in the end, all national differences, and constituting of all mankind one great brotherhood of nations."[2] It was a bit of irony that the steam engine, seen by many as a violent mechanical contrivance, should at the same time become a symbol for domestic peace and harmony. Americans hoped that the thing Charles Dickens called a "mad dragon" would ensure the gentle arts of peace.

Promoters believed, however, that the locomotive, like world peace and domestic tranquility, was a sign of a higher civilization. At least Poor asserted that "the locomotive engine has in twenty years become the great agent of civilization and progress, the most powerful instrument for good the world has yet reached, and become the most effective messenger for proclaiming peace on earth and good will to men." He wrote just after Christmas: "The age of locomotion is the era of progress—Wherever the railway extends, knowledge and civilization advance in geometrical ratio."

By establishing a ratio between the degree of civilization and miles of railway or numbers of locomotives, Poor created a new scale by which Americans could compare themselves to the old world. On that basis his countrymen took great delight in pointing out that the United States eclipsed Britain in almost all pertinent railway statistics, therefore proving once again the rightness of the Yankees' political experiment. Steamboats, railroads, and the telegraph, he wrote, "all the product of the last fifty years, will overthrow despotisms of the past, and reconstruct society on the principles of liberty and social order."[3]

Years later Walt Whitman distilled the essence of the steam locomotive's allure down to a single line in his poem "To a Locomotive in Winter," when he wrote: "Type of modern — emblem of motion and power — pulse of the continent."[4] A long-forgotten poet did the same at greater length in the early 1850s:

> For Lo! We live in an Iron Age —
> In the age of Steam and Fire!
> The world is too busy for dreaming,
> And hath grown too wise for war:
> So, to-day, for the glory of Science,
> Let us sing of the *Railway Car*![5]

Even editor Minor, who usually resisted the more outlandish metaphorical flourishes, fell under the spell of locomotive imagery in 1846 when he observed "we are preeminently a locomotive people and our very amusements are locomotive — the greater the speed, the greater the sport." He was sure, he said, that "they are perfectly in accordance with the genius of our people." His successor in the editor's chair was of like mind; seven years later Poor nudged the notion farther along when he claimed that "of all the members which compose the body of the railway, the *locomotive* is probably the nearest perfected."[6]

Americans' identification with their engines was prodded in part because locomotives took on physical characteristics that marked them as peculiarly American; no other nation's locomotives looked quite like them. Poor could remember steam engines when they were small crude contraptions, with vertical boilers that resembled nothing so much as oversize teakettles, all patterned on their English parents. The early engines, bearing such quaint names as *Jenny Lind, Bourbon, Atlas, Mercury, Miles Standish, Cyclops, Factory*

Girl, Antelope, and *Pioneer,* were almost miniatures, rattling over cast-iron strap rails with no protection for their crews and very little safety for their passengers. When locomotives became longer, more graceful, with attractively curved smokestacks, ornate wooden cabs, outsized headlights, fine brasswork, and painted detail, they became American works of art and acquired those peculiar attributes that marked them as native: inside frames with all their functional appurtenances hung on the outside of the engine. While their intricate valve gears, steam chests, cylinders, water pipes, sand domes, and everything else, including the most arresting American gadget of all, the cowcatcher, struck many as homely, they were cheaper to build that way and easier to repair in a land where function counted for more than looks.

It was those peculiar looks, however, that helped nurture the iron horse metaphor. The locomotive was an object of great interest, but at the same time it was outsized, noisy, hot, dangerous, smelly, and mysterious. There was the suspicion that a country founded upon Jeffersonian agrarian principles had bought a ticket and boarded a train pulled by some iron monster into the dark recesses of an unknown future. The journey may have been made in the name of progress, but it was still scary.

To ease such public apprehensions, promoters, poets, editors, and writers alike adopted the notion that locomotives were really only "iron horses," an early metaphor that lingered because it made steam technology ordinary and understandable. Promoters succeeded in making the exotic commonplace. In so doing, they lessened the tension between the nation's rural past and its technological future; the metaphor bridged the widening chasm between what America had been and what it was becoming. The practical result of the metaphorical construct was to encourage public enthusiasm for the new form of transportation. The machine steamed into the garden in the guise of an animal that had long browsed there.

Henry David Thoreau from his semi-seclusion at Walden watched the Fitchburg Railroad intrude on his Eden and with his sharp eye for detail and penchant for metaphor seized immediately upon the locomotive as an interloper. "That devilish Iron Horse, whose ear-rending whinner is heard throughout the town," he complained, "has defiled the Boiling Spring with his feet and drunk it up, and browsed

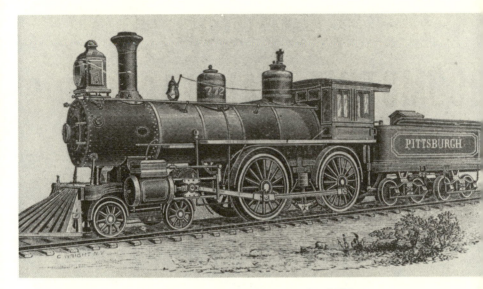

A fine example of a post Civil War
passenger locomotive with typically American accouterments.
(*Poor's Manual, 1889*)

on all the wood around the pond." Thoreau noted that "he has got a taste for berries even, and with unnatural appetite he robs the country babies of milk, with the breath of his nostrils polluting the air." He was, Thoreau concluded, "that Trojan horse, with a thousand men in his belly," and finally, "this bloated pest." While Thoreau was not wholly taken with locomotives' charms, he minimized their encroachment into his private world by metaphorically creating an animal that rightfully belonged there.[7]

Others less perspicacious could also mold something commonplace from the foreign. The Springfield (Massachusetts) *Gazette* editors printed a story in 1847 about a locomotive that ran away after its crew stepped off for a moment. The astounded engineer chased his engine on foot for miles, then commandeered a horse and finally caught his engine eleven miles down the track. Certainly chastened by the incident, the engineer got up steam again and brought the train back into Springfield. The moral of the story as the editors remarked, was "so much for leaving a *horse* in the street, without being made fast."[8]

Most thoughtful folk who expanded the iron horse's metaphorical possibilities were bolder than Thoreau and the Springfield editors. Usually they portrayed their "horse" as somewhat larger than life, bred of equal parts of machine, animal, fantasy and reality. Elihu Burritt, who founded the League of Universal Brotherhood in the 1840s and promoted the Second Universal Peace Congress held in Brussels in 1848, was taken by the iron horse metaphor.

> I love to see one of these huge creatures, with sinews of brass and muscles of iron, strut forth from his smoky stable, saluting the long train of cars with a dozen sonorous puffs from his iron nostrils, fall gently back into his harness. There he stands, champing and foaming upon the iron track, his great heart a furnace of glowing coals; his lymphatic blood is boiling in his veins; the strength of a thousand horses is nerving his sinews — he pants to be gone. He would "Snake" St. Peter's across the desert of Sahara, if he could be fairly hitched to it, but there is a little sober eyed, tobacco chewing man in the saddle, who holds him in with one finger, and can take away his breath in a moment, should he grow restive and vi-

cious . . . I regard him as the genius of the whole machinery, as the physical mind of that huge steam horse.[9]

An anonymous author in *Putnam's Monthly Magazine* tried his hand with the metaphor in 1853 and came up with a larger-than-life version. In a passage reminiscent of a Norse saga, he depicted the locomotive as "the Iron Horse, the earthshaker, the fire-breather, which tramples down the hills, which outruns the laggard winds, which leaps over the rivers, which grinds the rocks to powder and breaks down the gates of the mountains," adding, "he too shall build an empire and an epic." Fearing his readers were not yet impressed with his iron steed's accomplishments, the writer pressed on: "Shall not cities be formed from his vaporous breath, and men spring up from the cinders of his furnace?"

> Imagine, then, the vulcan-wrought engine rushing from sea to sea, dispensing lightening from its sides and thunder from its wheels — the one-eyed smiths from the doors of their workshops in the mountain, watching the progress of the prodigy with grim delight! [10]

Such sentiments were not confined to any literary set; men of a more practical bent saw the locomotive in the same terms. Witness Horatio Allen, the chief engineer of the South Carolina Canal and Rail-Road Company in the early 1830s, who came to New York in 1851 to speak at the opening of the New York and Erie Railroad. Allen suggested in his talk that if he had the power to view the future of railways in the United States he would see "a thousand iron horses starting forth from the various railroad centres, or traversing the surface of the continent in all directions." By contrast, in his first days as an engineer in South Carolina "only one of these iron monsters was in existence on this continent, and was moving forth, the first of his mighty race."[11]

The Charleston *Courier's* reporter, who was a passenger on the inaugural run of the *Best Friend of Charleston* on Christmas Day 1830, had used the iron horse metaphor on that occasion. As he saw it, "the iron horse 'Best Friend' was entered for the purse, about a fortnight since, to 'run against time.'" "Doubts were at first entertained as to 'his wind,' when everybody acknowledged he had sufficient 'bottom.'" He noted that "the 'Best Friend' is out of a horse

The *Best Friend of Charleston* performing for
the *Courier's* reporter on Christmas Day, 1830.
(Historical Pictures Service, Chicago)

bred by Messrs. Watt & Bolton, and of the same breed as Novelty and Rocket, which contended for the purse of £500, at the late Liverpool and Manchester races. By crossing the breed with a Columbian sire, he has 'eclipsed' his progenitors upon the European, and stands unrivalled upon the American turf." After the "race" the newsman admitted that "all doubts . . . of his being 'short winded' have been dissipated, and it is now confidently believed that he can run one hundred miles without 'flagging.'"[12]

There was a body of metaphorical literature that plainly crossed over the line into the absurd. Iron horses that "breathed vapors," "exhaled smoke," emitted "unearthly" noises, and vented their "shrieking" whistles conjured up visions of monsters, demons, and dragons. Usually such monsters were left undefined as if everybody knew exactly what a monster looked like. James Lanman, however, writing in *Hunt's Merchants' Magazine* in 1840 was more specific. He thought locomotives "dragons of mightier power, with iron muscles that never tire, breathing smoke and flame through their blackened lungs, feeding upon wood and water, out-running the race horse." He characterized the entire train "leaping forward like some black monster, upon its iron path, by the light of the fire and smoke which it vomits forth."[13]

Thoreau even saw dragons at his pond. He admitted in *Walden* he was not really sure what he saw, but thought it had all the earmarks of one. He wrote, "when I hear the iron horse make the halls echo with his snort like thunder, shaking the earth with his feet, and breathing fire and smoke from his nostrils, (what kind of winged horse or fiery dragon they will put into the new Mythology I don't know), it seems as if the earth had got a race now worthy to inhabit it." An unknown poet later mixed Thoreau's two images when he penned: "Be they warned when they hear the shrieking / Of the Dragon with Iron wings!"[14] Winged dragons represented speed and fire, as good a symbol as any for the locomotive.

In 1848 the Boston and Maine ran a trial between Lawrence and Pemberton with an engine suitably named *Antelope.* The locomotive started with a "terrific amount of snorting and a shower of sparks" and soon reached speed. When the train passed through the village of Reading, "the village drunkard took one look at the demon that streaked across his vision and was strictly sober for a fortnight thereafter."[15]

Nathaniel Hawthorne in his "The Celestial Railroad" was interested in railways' moral effects, but he used the same metaphor as the Reading village drunk. When the tale's main character prepared to board the train for a ride to the Celestial City, he took the time to note that "the engine at this moment took its station in advance of the cars, looking, I must confess, much more like a sort of mechanical demon that would harry us to the infernal regions than a laudable contrivance for smoothing our way to the Celestial City." Hawthorne used the demon metaphor as the main theme of his story. And he carried it further, indicating that "on its top sat a personage almost enveloped in smoke and flame, which, not to startle the reader, appeared to gush from its own mouth and stomach as well as from the engine's brazen abdomen." Mr. Smooth-it-away, a company director, explained that the engineer was Apollyon, a monster in John Bunyan's *Pilgrim's Progress* "clothed with scales like fish" and having "wings like a dragon, feet like a bear," while "out of his belly came fire and smoke" and "his mouth was as the mouth of a lion."[16]

This was the locomotive's metaphorical dark side, but the most hideous metaphors were always overwhelmed in the public prints by a swarm of homely metaphors that mitigated the more monstrous excesses. Thoreau, for example, used a domestic image to describe the locomotive as a "boiling, sizzling kettle," although he also noted the passengers "make me think of potatoes, which a fork would show to be done by this time." He eschewed the fire-snorting image; instead he saw that "the steam is denser for the cold, and more white; like the purest downy clouds in the summer sky, its volumes roll up between me and the moon."[17] He continued with the mundane imagery in *Walden*:

> The stabler of the iron horse was up early this winter morning by the light of the stars amid the mountains, to fodder and harness his steed. Fire, too, was awakened thus early to put the vital heat in him and get him off. If the enterprise were as innocent as it is early! If the snow lies deep, they strap on his snowshoes, and with the giant plough, plough a furious furrow from the mountains to the seaboard, in which the cars,

like a following drill-barrow, sprinkle all the restless men and floating merchandise in the country for seed. All day the fire-steed flies over the country, stopping only that his master may rest, and I am awakened by his tramp and defiant snort at midnight, when in some remote glen in the woods he fronts the elements incased in ice and snow; and he will reach his stall only with the morning star, to start once more on his travels without rest or slumber. Or perchance, at evening, I hear him in his stable blowing off the superfluous energy of the day, that he may calm his nerves and cool his liver and brain for a few hours of iron slumber.[18]

Nothing frightening or monstrous here. The loudest report he noted was only a "defiant snort." The steam engine enjoyed a happy domestic routine that was as endless and repetitive as that of the human race.

Walt Whitman, although not as captivated by railroads and their iron horses as Thoreau, did note the intruder in his garden several times. Whitman was much less apprehensive about the new technological era than most literary figures of his generation; no frightening mechanical monstrosities for him. Instead, in his "Poem of Joys" written in 1860 he pointed out the invention's happy nature:

O the engineer's joys!
To go with a locomotive!
To hear the hiss of steam — the merry shriek — the steam-whistle — the laughing locomotive!
To push with resistless way, and speed off in the distance.[19]

Ralph Waldo Emerson saw the locomotive as an agent for domestic harmony. In 1844 when the controversies over slavery and Texas were tying national political figures in Gordian knots, he looked across the continent, certain that he had a way to cut through them "to hold the Union Staunch." He observed that "the locomotive and the steamboat, like enormous shuttles, shoot every day across the thousand various threads of national descent and employment and bind them fast in one web," adding "an hourly assimilation goes forward, and there is no danger that local peculiarities and hostilities should be preserved." Jotting in his journal at the end of the Mexican War, Emerson returned to the problem of national unity,

After seeing steam engines like the *West Point*,
Emerson could dream of holding the Union together
and linking the coasts by rail.
(Historical Pictures Service, Chicago)

"The timeliness of this invention of the locomotive must be conceded," he decided. "To us Americans, it seems to have fallen as a political aid. We could not else have held the vast North America together, which now we engage to do." A scant three years later, soon after the Compromise of 1850 had deflated sectional passions, Emerson cryptically noted that "the Railroad & Telegraph are great unionists."[20]

It is illustrative of Emerson's broad metaphorical outlook on the world that he could look at a locomotive and not notice its machinery and behavior. He chose instead to concentrate on the continental role it would play in bringing the American people together. "It was strange, too," he pointed out, "that when it was time to build a road to the Pacific, a railroad, a shiproad, a telegraph, and, in short, a perfect communication in every manner for all nations, —'twas to see how it was secured." To the New England philosopher, the locomotive was the perfect adjunct to a rampant Manifest Destiny.[21]

The pot of gold at Sutter's Mill was about as far as the iron horse metaphor could have been stretched. The iron horse and the gold rush came together after the Mexican War to create a national mood of optimism, even in the midst of the heated slavery debates. Americans, with their metaphorical locomotives, had harnessed and controlled nature on a continental scale. Powerful images of a people strong, fast, and "on track" seemed to promise progress and a bright future. At the same time the metaphor helped to scale down the immensity of the new invention and "tamed" its more threatening aspects by stabling the iron horse in a metaphorical barnyard. It promised Americans that science and time were on their side.

And sing to the Glory of Science —
  Exult in the downfall of war — [1]

CHAPTER 3

No More War

├─┼─┼─┼─┼─┼─┼─┼─┼─┼─┼─┼─┼─┼─┼─┤

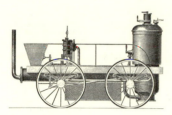

Wᴴᴇɴ the Baltimore and Ohio and the Charleston and Hamburg laid their first rails, the country had been independent only slightly more than half a century. In that short time it had fought two wars with Great Britain, an undeclared war with France, and constant battles with the Indians. None of these conflicts had been easy, and Americans sought a means to achieve internal unity to counterbalance further external dangers. And although the nation was at peace except for the Indian wars, for the first two decades of railroad construction promoters assumed in their literature that more wars were sure to follow. Even America's favorable geographical position — shielded by two oceans from the worst foreign entanglements — which gave it a degree of absolute security rare in the world, failed to quell its uneasiness about its military weakness.

To further compound their fears, Americans also faced a unique security problem; as they expanded across the continent, they daily became increasingly vulnerable. Their nation's borders were always longer, more remote, less defensible, and frequently more ill defined. The problems of defending the ever-changing boundaries were monumental, especially in a country dedicated to the principle of relying upon a citizens' militia. To defend what even then Americans referred to as their "empire," they feared they would have to dispatch permanent garrisons to all frontiers and build a bigger navy for the Atlantic and Gulf ports. Both would be expensive and the idea of large standing military forces appalled many only a generation removed from the Revolution. Railroad enthusiasts had the perfect answer to such apprehensions, and their metaphors that emphasized both mobility and constriction had a powerful appeal to those who worried about such things.

Talented railroad promoters took the defense metaphor and wound it tightly back into its larger national unity image. They pointed out that their projects would make the nation internally more secure and therefore ready to move its small mobile force quickly along the rails to thwart any aggressor. The nation could safely draw together while spreading out. Early advocates detailed specific points that railroads would guard and even painted possible invasion scenarios that could only have served to increase their readers' fears. As the rails reached out into the hinterlands, however, promoters by the early 1840s began to trace defensive railway systems that would secure the safety of all regions.

Advocates were not blind to the self-serving aspects of their defense arguments. From the 1820s they recognized that if they could promote their projects as essential to the nation's defense they stood a good chance of enticing federal funds into their coffers. Their appeals were not wholly selfish; the notion that their companies could serve the nation's welfare and their own was fully consistent with the national unity image. Railway enthusiasts appealed to their fellow countrymen's insecurities early. In 1829 a committee in Baltimore, representing its fellow townfolk who a scant fifteen years earlier had suffered from America's weakness when the British fleet approached their harbor, pulled the elements of the unity image together. Calling for public help to construct the B&O, the committee voiced its confidence that "this government will not withhold its aid when we thus most effectually . . . secure the rapid movement and concentration of troops and military stores in war, . . . and give permanancy to the union."[2]

Two months earlier, William Jackson, a member of the Massachusetts Charitable Mechanics Association, delivered a "lecture on Rail Roads" and dealt in part with the contributions railroads would make to the nation's defense. Sometimes he sounded surprisingly modern. "There is an old maxim," he remembered, "in times of peace prepare for war. The usual preparation for war, however," he continued, "has had such a tendency to produce an appetite for it, that this has of late become a maxim of doubtful cast." Advocating the "visionary" construction of a road from Albany to Boston, Jackson argued that spending 3 million dollars on it "would do more to preserve us from that calamity, or sustain us under it, than ten millions for a navy. Indeed," he was certain that "if there is any one measure doing more than all others to render us as a nation invulnerable, it is that of our internal improvements."[3]

The Pennsylvania legislature's Inland Navigation Committee took a higher view of the whole subject in 1830, noting that "people who are their own masters, bestow their attention and means on the arts of peace and comfort, rather than the works of hostility, extravagance, and ostentation." Its members concluded with the observation that "the ways of internal improvements are ways of pleasantness, and all their paths are peace." Dr. Caldwell, lecturing in Boston two years later agreed. "The certain prevention of foreign war, therefore, from violating our borders, and the foot of a foe from insulting our soil, will be one of the numerous advantages of Rail-roads," he prophesied, not without flair. Continuing, he expanded his purview, "Indeed, the invention will do much towards the suppression of war in general — a thousand fold more than all the Peace and Missionary Societies that will ever be established." Caldwell, like most Americans, was less certain about the elimination of war than his rhetoric indicated, for elsewhere in his talk he rhapsodized:

> What hostile force will dare to approach such a moral volcano, whose slumbering fires the first breath of war would awaken to fierce and desolating action! With the expedition of magic, the whole embodied prowess and power, and all the military enginery of the nation, might be brought to bear on any single point, to discomfit and destroy an approaching enemy.

Caldwell's sentiments were strikingly contemporary. Railroads were such a powerful new weapon that they would surely deter anyone from attacking the United States; they would bring permanent peace in their wake.[4]

The editor of the *Niles' Register* had said virtually the same thing, but doubted the effectiveness of America's fighting force once it arrived at the front. Niles was certain, however, "we would, in the event of war, be able, in a very few hours, or at most in two or three days, to concentrate the whole disposable force of the country on a single point, either for attack or defence." But he was also thinking in terms of retreat, adding, "of such a resource, an invading force could never avail himself, since a road could be rendered impassable in a few moments by those who occupy the country." Thirty odd years later the Confederate military leaders made just such a notion reality.[5]

Railroad advocates drew upon American experiences in the War of 1812 to frame their arguments. They found an almost unlimited number of illustrations, as the United States military had not exactly covered itself with glory in that conflict. The Louisiana state legislature reminded its fellow citizens in 1832 that, with the new railways, "in time of war, our only risk by capture, would be . . . the foreign trade," and pointed out that during the last conflict the enemy had seized coastal vessels carrying as much as "two-thirds or more of the agricultural product." The solons then drove home their telling point: "It was in fact, paying and feeding the enemy while fighting him." A federal railroad linking the South with northern centers, the legislators argued, would help by providing "advantages in economy, and facilitating the operation of carrying on war." Moreover, then "a smaller force would be required to protect our extensive frontiers; but added to all these advantages," the Bayou Staters concluded, it would have the "happy effect" of "amalgamating our interest and assimilating our habits and manners."[6]

Four years later General Edmund Pendleton Gaines, who had firsthand knowledge of military history in the War of 1812 and the First Seminole War, wrote to the editor of the *American Railroad Journal* predicting that the U.S. Navy would be beaten in the next war. That catastrophe did not appear to bother the old general much, for he also believed that "our railroads and canals costing not more for each hundred miles than a first rate ship of the line, would endure unhurt the pelting of a thousand storms, and would forever stand as a glorious monument to the wisdom, enterprise, and energy of Oliver Evans, Robert Fulton, DeWitt Clinton, and their followers." The veteran could accept the prospect of a naval defeat as long as his country built its railroads. "We should then see," he prophesied, "the *sugar, cotton, rice, coffee, lead, and iron* and other valuable products of the south and west, with thousands of passengers of the south and west, flying under the giant grasp of steam power with its thousand cars per day." Let the enemies have the seas, the nation's march to its destiny would continue unabated.[7]

Politicians and army generals were not the only people to read their history; common folks could just as easily graft the lessons of the past to the prevailing national image. In fact a crowd at a 1835 public meeting held in Cincinnati to agitate for a railway from that river town to Charleston, South Carolina, noted in its appeal that "no public work could contribute more powerfully to our national defence." It would, argued those attending, "present a new triumph of civilization over barbarism, by making civil public works, an efficient substitute for standing armies and powerful navies, which exhaust the resources and endanger the liberties of a nation." The Cincinnati convention did not pinpoint a specific foreign threat, but it had a domestic one in mind. It promised that after their railroad was built, "the north [*sic*] and South would, in fact, shake hands with each other, yield up their social and political hostility, pledge themselves to common national interests, and part as friends and brethren." Anticipating the demographic patterns of the next century, the convention pointed out that Yankees would flock to the balmy southern climes on the new railroad in the winter, "catching a glow of southern feeling, gratifying their curiosity, and return enlarged in their patriotism and enriched in their knowledge of our common country."[8]

The promoters who wrote the prospectus for the Illinois Central Railroad also understood the connection between defense expenditures and availability of public monies for their project. After opening with the pronouncement that their road "unquestionably is of greater importance to . . . the whole Union than any similar work yet projected," they turned to exploit the public's fear of national weakness by declaring "in a short space of time any number of troops, with all the necessary munitions of war, could be transported from one section of the country to the other, and such a facility of transportation would render unnecessary a large standing army, or expensive fortifications, in the west."⁹

Most promotional statements touting the railroads' contribution to the national defense were intentionally vague. The enemies remained unseen and unnamed; they were more frightening that way. George Farquhar's speech on the opening of the Pottsville and Philadelphia Railroad in 1842, for example, was typical in that he mentioned only that the road would "increase our domestic comforts and protect us from foreign aggression," very much like an earlier anonymous writer's afterthought that with a railroad, "the tremendous resources of this extensive country could be brought almost with the speed of wind to defend any point of attack."

A few writers, however, warned more specifically of the Indian menace. It appeared to be an iron law that the closer one came to the frontier, the less vague and general became his references to foreign aggression and national defense. When the Wisconsin Railroad Committee, for example, sent letters to Congress almost ten years before that territory became a state, its members were nervous about their vulnerable position on the nation's flank and certain of what railroads could do for their security. And they did not mince their words, maintaining that "this Road would afford to the United States a most efficient and economical check upon the vast hordes of savage Indians, congregating to so formidable extent upon her exposed and widely spread northwestern frontier, and would prove of paramount utility in the not impossible event of a foreign invasion." Unlike their eastern countrymen who worried about more distant menaces, the Wisconsin settlers wanted railroads to help increase the national military presence in their backyard. They promoted their project as one designed to carry U.S. "troops, military stores, and munitions of war, for the various permanent garrisons now existing, and to be further increased in the Indian country." Like most Americans of the era, however, the promoters also looked beyond their immediate wants and proclaimed that national greatness would naturally follow if their particular improvement were constructed. The Wisconsin writers allowed their imaginations to roam freely into the future, boasting that their road "would constitute a permanent link in the great Oregon Railroad, which the indomitable spirit of American enterprise will, at no distant day,

This was what George Farquhar had in mind
to defend America's most remote frontiers.
(Brown, *The History of the First Locomotives in America*)

exhibit to an admiring world, connecting our Atlantic with our Pacific sea-board."[10]

The Wisconsin promoters' transcontinental visions predated Asa Whitney's untiring promotion of a similar project the following decade. By the 1840s even advocates back East saw the advantages of such a road for dealing with the Indians. The editor of the *American Railroad Journal*, after an initial hesitation, caught the transcontinental fever in 1845 when he penned an editorial, "The Oregon Railway," that began with the eye-catching phrase: "Listen to that unearthly sound, the *steam whistle* of the locomotive, as the engineer gives warning to the astonished herds of Buffalo that are grazing upon the track in advance of the train." He then became more serious. With conflict heating up on the nation's southwestern border, he argued, and "with the thirst for more territory by her [Mexico's] politicians, and consequently the necessity imposed upon the government for providing for the defense of our territory on the Pacific, which is to be the great *battlefield of universal freedom* to mankind, the U.S. had better build the road." It was not the "Asian peril" that bothered Minor; rather, he thought it would be "from the shores of the Pacific ocean that the monarchial governments of the old world will attempt, if they deign *ever to make the effort,* to arrest the progress, or to suppress the existence of republican institutions."[11]

Minor was not alone in regarding railroads as a frontier defense against European depredations. The Cincinnati *Daily Chronicle* published a long piece in 1843 that included the flat assertion: "There is a constant tendency among us to controversy; . . . a war with Great Britain is almost inevitable." The fact that there were no immediate crises with the mother country that year did not for a moment deter the nervous railroad promoter-editor. He concluded: "It is of vast importance that we have main lines of permanent railroad, extending from the principal cities to the *interior,* to the *frontier,* to the *far west,* that troops, provisions, and munitions of war may be transported rapidly from place to place." Having thus safeguarded his country's physical integrity, the author was certain the railways also would be "dispelling prejudices and cementing friendships, calculated to perpetuate the institutions under which we have risen from a mere handful, and are *growing to be* the *mightiest* nation on earth."[12]

Even as Americans looked back at the mistakes they made in the last war and bemoaned their military impotence, they had their eyes cocked on the future. Americans were convinced that with railways the country was set firmly on the path to becoming one of the world's premier powers. The editor of the Albany *Argus* unburdened himself of such sentiments in an 1845 article on railroads' beneficent effects. After paying homage to the national unity image, reiterating that "the impulse which leads to the linking of the iron bands of brotherhood and union is a noble one," the editorialist took up the issues of defense and destiny. "Though railroads are one of the strongest and most enduring arms of peace," he punned, "they immeasureably strengthen the military efficiency of our country and add to its national greatness and power in the eyes of the world."[13]

The biggest obstacle to achieving such goals, many thought, was that the United States was growing so fast, extending its borders so rapidly, that it was becoming weaker at its extremities. At the same time many Americans feared an attack on eastern cities — a danger, no matter how remote, that multiplied the government's defense problems. Railway promoters had the answers. "We are a stirring people," Minor declared in something of an understatement, "spread over a vast territory, and need, more than any other country, the facilities afforded by railroads . . . especially to improve our means of *defence in case of invasion or insurrection.*" A month later, in February 1846, Asa Whitney presented Congress with yet another of his petitions for financial help to construct a transcontinental. After dangling the mercantile lure that such a road would capture the trade of 700 million Chinese souls, he went on to outline the military advantages of his project. He pointed out that "the people of Oregon are now claiming the care and protection of our government, which cannot now be extended to them. Therefore," he continued, "without this road, Oregon must become a separate nation, or belong to some of the powers of Europe, commanding the commerce of the world, and our most dangerous rivals."[14]

Railroad boosters did not have to look all the way out to Oregon, however, to raise alarm over the safety of the nation's frontiers. Dangers lurked everywhere. A writer for the *National Intelligencer* expressed doubts about the ability of the country to defend even the southern Mississippi Valley and advocated the construction of what he called a "Great Chain of Southern Railroads," arguing that with such communications, "in a *military point of view* Tennessee and Kentucky will ever be found ready to afford assistance in time of war to their more exposed brethren." The author, beset by all manner of fears, asked, "Might not Charleston at some day need the same defenders as New Orleans? Are not both the south and the northwest interested in receiving aid *by the shortest and most expeditious route*, in case of sudden invasion?, or in case of insurrection might be added." The *American Railroad Journal*'s editor loved answering those questions; he supported building a New Orleans to Washington, D.C., railroad, pointing out that "in no way, it appears to us, can so much be accomplished in the way of defence and at the same time for the general business of the country, as by the construction of railroads — as they will be found efficient in war and still more so in times of peace, without being a burthen to the people."[15]

By April 1846 it was apparent to all that war with Mexico was a distinct probability. United States troops had marched to the north bank of the Rio Grande, occupied disputed territory, and were glaring across the river at their Mexican counterparts. John Slidell's mission to settle the dispute by purchasing parts of Mexico was a predictable failure, and sabers were rattling in both capitals. In the midst of all the clamor, a Pennsylvania representative, Andrew Stewart, stood up and delivered a masterful speech to Congress that summed up many of the enthusiasts' military arguments and placed them in a political context designed to appeal to southerners. His theme was simple: "As a means of national defence a general system of railroads, connecting our cities on the seaboard and penetrating the interior, was better and more effectual in an extended country like ours than any system of fortifications that could be devised." And Stewart had a sense of history, reminding his audience that "had we possessed such roads last war, this city [Washington] would never have fallen into the hands of the enemy; . . . and they never would have wrapped the capitol in flames." The congressman, an early supporter of the Chesapeake and Ohio Canal, knew the value of promotion and applied the lessons he had learned earlier. "In times of peace forts are useless; costing millions to erect them, they are utterly without value," he declared, while "railroads are as useful in peace as in war." The Whig representative appealed to his southern colleagues to vote for federal aid to a railway from Washington to New Orleans with the argument that "if railroads are a better means of defence than forts, then they are more constitutional, being more 'necessary and proper' for carrying out the defensive powers conferred upon congress." Stewart's argument for military necessity, economy, usefulness, and constitutionality, however well contrived, was insufficient to wring funds from Congress; the government had a war to worry about.[16]

Farther south, DeBow, editor of the highly respected *DeBow's Review*, was promoting the Southern Atlantic and Mississippi Railway, and his rhetoric was very similar to Stewart's. After claiming that his road "would furnish means of throwing down upon the Atlantic coasts, in thirty-six hours, during war, for the common defense, any number of stout hearts and strong arms for the distant West," he quoted extensively from James Gadsden's report on the project. Gadsden, destined to become a textbook name after his purchase of a bit of Mexico for a transcontinental route, gave the usual nod to the need for military transportation and then pointed out that such a development would enable "one army to defend two frontiers, and one crew to serve two fleets, as an enemy may either threaten the Atlantic or Gulf frontier. It gives us as the basis of operations the Chord, while the enemy has the arc of the circle to move on his demonstrations of attack." Obviously practiced in the fine art of persuasion, he continued to expound on "the magical power of steam, it gives wings to our arms, and enables us . . . to realize the great problem of military success—'*Concentration of force and celerity of movement.*'"[17]

Oddly enough, when war was declared on Mexico on May 11, 1846, promoters, with few exceptions, ignored it. Few Americans thought the war was a national crisis, and enlistments were low. Many assumed that railroads and canals could carry necessary war materials and troops along with their normal traffic without undue strain. If the war affected U.S. railways at all, it was in that it revealed sharply the gaps that existed between roads stretching from the Atlantic Coast into the Southwest. Many of those bottlenecks, however, remained when the next war broke out fifteen years later. The war slowed rail construction. The conflict began just as the 1839 depression was beginning to lift in New England. People there were not very avid supporters of Mr. Polk's war anyway, and they concentrated their resources instead on building those projects they had been forced to postpone for years. New England promoters' biggest concern was how to raise funds to bring their plans off the drawing boards. In wartime, with a nation just emerging from its worst depression, that was no mean task.

The *American Railroad Journal,* a public forum for promoters' plans, pleas, dreams, and excuses, while certainly not a political newspaper, announced the war in an even more oblique manner than usual by burying it in the middle of a discussion of the Southern Railroad of Mississippi. That road's enthusiasts promised to build a link connecting Georgia to the Mississippi at Vicksburg, and Minor strongly applauded their efforts. "It is a matter of vast importance," he editorialized "not only to the people of that region, but . . . to the United States government, in times like the present, when its gallant little army is within an enemy's territory." He obviously expected American arms to triumph, for he added, almost as an aside, "with a continuous railroad to the Mississippi, ample reinforcements and munitions might be sent to their aid if deemed necessary."[18]

Not until three issues later did Minor ever get around to mentioning the war again. This time he generously devoted a whole editorial, "War and the Railroads," to the subject to quell rumors currently flying that the Mexicans might attack American port cities. He explained that as long as any city was connected to its interior by rail it was safe and pointed out that since New York City had no rail connection with Albany it would be vulnerable as soon as the Hudson iced over. He warmed to his subject by noting that "the military value of railways is attracting the attention of all European powers, as we have declared ourselves, *the* great American power — as we have through our rulers thrown down the gauntlet to the world." That was as much patriotic rhetoric as Minor could muster — a strange reticence for a man who had published so many treatises on railroads and national defense. Presumably he was only lukewarm in support of American intervention in Mexican affairs.[19]

In the West, where proximity to the fighting sharpened attitudes, the St. Louis *New Era* evinced surprise that "a slight war with a feeble nation has thrown the commerce of the west in a state of ruinous confusion." As one of the principal military entrepots, St. Louis was in chaos. In explaining the reasons to their readers, the editors betrayed deep-seated fears of that "feeble nation." "If we had good railroads to the east," they whined, "the commerce of the west would not be thus injured and prostrated. Internal lines of communication would render us more safe and independent. The alarm and panic of war would be stripped of a part of their terrors by the construction of railroads to the Atlantic."[20]

Paradoxically, the war at least temporarily ended the promoters' emphasis on military defense. Most railroadmen such as J. Edgar Thomson, the chief engineer of the Georgia Railroad, looked at the war in practical terms. He predicted in May that "this Mexican war will give us a lift in the way of travel" on his Montgomery and West Point road. Traffic everywhere was rising, profits were increasing, and capital for new projects was forthcoming. As the war with Mexico wound its way to what most Americans considered was its foregone conclusion, railway publicists played down the military advantages and instead emphasized their proposals' commercial benefits. Roebling, the German-born genius who would span Niagara Gorge with an engineering marvel, illustrated this new outlook when he promoted his "Great Central Railroad from Philadelphia to St. Louis" early in 1847. Amazingly, in the middle of a war he could write that "one of the best proofs of the advancement of mankind in *true* civilizations is, that the industrial efforts of nations are no longer squandered upon the creation of vast monuments of pride and war." Instead, he argued, railroads were creating wealth and "like a magic wand" they could open "slumbering resources and long hidden treasures of the earth; convert stone and iron into gold."[21]

The irony of the national defense arguments was that only after they were abandoned were the promoters' earlier boasts proved accurate. The Mexican War generals learned firsthand just how useful the new invention could be, and they took that knowledge into the

The *General Haupt*'s beauty belied its military function
in the Civil War.
(Author's collection)

Civil War, the first conflict fought with strategies and tactics designed to make maximum use of railways. But the divisive aspects of the Mexican War did not serve the national unity image, as promoters everywhere instinctively understood. The conflict exacerbated sectional and political divisions, and railroad advocates had more effective ammunition to deal with them. They preferred to emphasize positive images of what the character of their nation could be than to dwell on the public's manifold anxieties. One of their strongest, although least well-defined, suggestions was that railways would fulfill the promise Jefferson made in his Declaration of Independence and bring in their wake, to paraphrase his document, increased health, wealth, wisdom, and . . . happiness.

For Science has opened a broad highway
For Knowledge and Truth and Right

CHAPTER 4

"Diminishing the Stock of Human Misery"

⊢—┼—┼—┼—┼—┼—┼—┼—┼—┼—┼—┼—┼—┼—┤

A correspondent who could not resist the temptation to pun, wrote the *American Railroad Journal* in February 1832 about some matter that he said "has given rise to a train of reflection." Unknowingly the writer had stumbled upon one of the industry's most important contributions to the national unity image: railroads would spread the knowledge essential to America's preservation and prosperity and to the determination of its character. Over the next two decades promoters argued that an unschooled and ignorant citizenry was likely to be poor, idle, and into mischief, all of which led to immorality and ultimately to loss of personal and national freedom. They further reasoned that the poor and ignorant were often unhealthy and that such people were also apt to be immoral. The sheer bulk of this literature illustrates the advocates' grave doubts about the moral underpinnings of the nation.[1]

Americans had long been stung by Europeans' conception of them as country bumpkins, unlettered, frequently unwashed, and without culture, cuisine, literature, or manners. However much foreign travelers might admire American institutions, inventiveness, impetuosity, frankness, and willingness to change, their charges that the new nation was somehow culturally and morally deficient were bitterly resented. Railway promoters exploited such indignation by pointing out that railroads hauled knowledge — and enlightenment, freedom, health, prosperity, and morality — in every train. Such cargoes, the enthusiasts agreed, could only uplift the country's moral character and raise its level of civilization.

Observers everywhere argued that the best antidote to political schism was the spread of common ideas; the continuation of the federal experiment was predicated upon the existence of a mass of like-thinking, but disputatious individuals with free and easy access to useful ideas and precepts. A fundamental impediment to achieving that ideal, however, was thought to lie in the fact that knowledge, culture, riches, and ideas radiated in a series of concentric circles from the coastal areas, becoming less compelling in each succeeding wave. Out on the frontiers, Americans' moral and intellectual fiber needed constant refreshment, especially, some thought, in the South and West, where heretical notions appeared to flourish. Railroad promoters discovered one of their strongest appeals was to allay national fears about intellectual malnourishment at the nation's fringes. They argued that their trains would carry the "liberal" ideas, usually found only in the cosmopolitan seaboard cities, into every backwoods hamlet in the land. Promoters engaged in a certain tautologous argument here; railroads, they asserted, the product of bright, forward-thinking inventors, would bring to everyone at least a passing acquaintance with the underlying knowledge that made such a wonderful invention possible in the first place. Indeed, the *idea* that railroads were a positive good and always in the nation's interest was itself a powerful unifying force.

The notion that railways were both physical manifestations of a new intellectual world and the means for making that world available to all citizens and, in the process, elevating the national character was one of the major reasons for the era's optimism. Observers, with charming naiveté, almost routinely observed that theirs was a "wonderfully progressive era." The whole of the Louisiana legislature agreed and predicted "the present age" would "be productive of wonderful events, as well in the sciences and mechanic arts, as in the principles of government and political economy." And the Bayou State lawmakers knew it was "on account of the rapid spread of knowledge, which is said to be a Nation's power," although they wondered aloud whether that power was not becoming too concentrated for the nation's good.[2]

As early as 1827 the Pennsylvania legislature's Committee on Inland Navigation recognized the relationship between rails, knowledge, and national harmony when it stated that "the utility of canal navigation and rail roads, in promoting industry and the free exchange of products of labor and the mind, is now universally acknowledged. . . . Next to the establishment of schools, . . . to give permanence to our free institutions, there is nothing more interesting than the perfection of the means of interior communication." When citizens could travel freely through the Keystone State, the committee averred, "it will consolidate the varied population of Pennsylvania into one great mass, influenced by the same interests and pointing its active energies to the same objects." A more thoughtful committee than most, it concluded that transportation "will call forth the resources of the commonwealth, and by furnishing a fund for education, will ultimately expand all its moral powers." Thus, committee members expected to dedicate profits from a public improvement to general education in order to unite all Pennsylvanians.[3]

The Inland Navigation Committee touched a sensitive national nerve. Although proud of their political experiment, Americans were concerned that the institutions they had nurtured were tenuous at best. By harping upon the subject, promoters showed that they shared these apprehensions. Unlike many Americans, however, they thought they had the answers and skillfully presented their projects as being the best defense against political backsliding. J. Kimball Minor wrote in 1843 "that the *monarchial* governments of Europe duly appreciate the vast importance of railroads as a means of controlling the people; but if we are not mistaken, *railroads* are the precursors of *liberty* and *equality* to the *people* everywhere." After placing railroads in the vanguard of efforts to preserve American institutions, Minor argued that the glue that bound them to freedom's defense was "intelligence" [that] leads directly to liberty and equality."[4]

Promoters who stressed railroads' contribution to the dissemination of knowledge were squarely in the mainstream of the Jeffersonian notion that an educated yeomanry was the best guarantee of the American experiment's success. The rail literature hints that an awful lot of Americans did not exactly fit the enlightened ideal, and one suspects that many promoters thought their countrymen little more than intellectual dwarfs and cultural oafs, but entertained high hopes that they were capable of being elevated to reasonable standards. Most railway enthusiasts were never that specific, however. They were usually content to advertise, as one did in *Niles' Register* in 1829, that railroads "most effectually promote the diffusion of intelligence." Others were less general; a local advocate, for example, wrote to the Onondaga (New York) *Standard*, "we all gain by the diffusion of knowledge — by the spread among us of useful inventions, and by various improvements which skill and enterprize produce. These are all stimulated by the railway."[5]

Numerous promoters knew exactly what the railways' diffusion of knowledge would do for the nation. The most common boasts were along the lines of those of a writer in the *Niles' Register* who observed that railroads would cause "distant schools of greater excellence [to be] brought into our domain." Caldwell, in his 1832 address, made the connection very specific. Railways, he thought, would lead to "an improvement in common school education. Parents becoming wealthier by it [presumably the railroad] will procure for their children more competent instructors. They will also continue longer at school. Thus will they cause them — by now he had completely lost his antecedent — "not only to be taught more correctly, but to be more thoroughly initiated in the elements of knowledge." And according to Caldwell, acquisition of knowledge had the most salutory effects; "that such measures will contribute to the promotion of sound morals, as well as of enlightened taste and becoming manners, will not be questions," he asserted, concluding that "they cannot indeed fail to ameliorate the entire condition of society."[6]

Caldwell also ventured the proposition that knowledge gives rise to more knowledge, an idea numerous promoters emphasized as well. Caldwell, however, did it better; railroads, he claimed, "will give rise to other inventions and improvements in mechanics. This they will do by stimulating the minds of gifted mechanicians to higher exertions. Men of genius are keenly ambitious." The good doctor had obviously given railroads and education a great deal of thought, for he had even chosen the "certain branches of science, the knowledge of which will be, . . . promoted . . . by the establishment of Railroads. These are, geography, . . . topography, mineral-ogy, geology, zoology, and botany." Summing it all up, he decided that "they all exercise a moral influence." Looking at the history of these disciplines, Caldwell was certainly not far wrong; engi-neering was the only field he missed.[7]

Not all Americans embraced the idea that railroads were a har-binger of a fabulously enlightened society. Ralph Waldo Emerson watched the Fitchburg Railroad construction crews pass within ear-shot of his house and thought about what it meant. When he wrote in his *Journal* in June 1847 that "railroads are to civilization what mathematics were to the mind," and "their immense promise made the whole world nervous with hope & fear," he appeared to be in wholehearted agreement with the thrust of promoters' arguments. He veered from the traveled path, however, when he claimed that railroads "leave society as they found it." None of the great dreams of "ramified, complex, and widely diffused" benefits for him. In-stead, he continued, "the man gets out of the railroad car at the end of 500 miles in every respect the same as he got in." And if that were not strong enough, he dealt the whole discussion of railroads and intelligence a telling blow with the simple addendum, "but a book or a friend opens a secret door at his side that may lead to Parnassus."[8]

Fortunately for the railroad business, however, not many Ameri-cans imbibed of Emerson's skepticism. Edward Everett, a Renais-sance man of the nineteenth century, one of the founders of the Boston Public Library and an 1860 vice-presidential candidate with John Bell, demonstrated his own faith when he offered a toast on July 6, 1835, at the opening of the Boston and Worcester Railroad. Hoisting his glass high, he intoned to the gathering: "The march of capital and enterprise — may it go hand in hand with the march of intellect and morals, and result in the increased prosperity and virtue of the people." Higher intellect as a prerequisite for morality had long been an article of faith in Enlightenment thinking; Ever-ett simply added the railway to the formula as a catalyst. The con-nection was almost a decade old when he made the toast, for as far back as 1827 Pennsylvania's Inland Navigation Committee prom-ised its state works "would increase the Commonwealth's moral powers."[9]

That a project contributed to the spread of morality might appear at first glance to be one of the weaker arguments promoters had in their oratorical arsenal, but their contemporaries did not think so. Even men who oversaw public funds often justified their expenditure on private projects in terms of the moral benefits all would enjoy. A special committee appointed by the Pennsylvania House of Representatives in 1839 to decide whether the state in those hard times should subscribe to the Sunbury and Erie Railroad's stock, for example, finally recommended a liberal subscription, admitting that it did not know "what would [be] the mere physical effects of this improvement," but asking that its members "may be allowed to express their belief, that the moral results would be far more gratifying and important." The committee backed up this strange assertion with specifics designed to persuade its audience: "Portions of the state, now comparatively wild and unproductive would . . . speedily be occupied by a dense population of intelligent freemen, . . . skilled in the arts of civilization, and refined moral and religious virtues, a prospect more pleasing to the philanthropist and patriot, *than the mere anticipation of profit to the public treasury.*" That conception of railroad's public utility would not long survive the Civil War, when the profit motive came to dominate other considerations. The pursuit of profits, however, set citizen against citizen, while the argument for railroads' higher morality and civilizing tendencies encouraged unity.[10]

Back in 1832, the Chester County, Pennsylvania, *Democrat* had made the same point as the house committee, but in a more folksy manner. The editor noted that "wherever the Railroad has passed, it has carried a stimulus to industry, displayed not only in solid and permanent improvements, but in attention to matters of comfort and ornament. Fences are put up or repaired, and arranged with neatness; garden palings are whitewashed; and fields before perhaps never turned with a plough, and long given to barrenness, are now broken up in readiness to receive the grain." These were perhaps only minor demonstrations of the rails' civilizing influence, but it is, after all, the many small touches that make life agreeable. That is what the editor of the *American Railroad Journal* was getting at the same year when he asked "whether this attempt to engraft the interests of business upon those of amusement, and to unite what is practically useful with what tends to embellish life, will be sustained." It was also the point being made by the New York Internal Improvement Convention which published in 1836 a letter with eight reasons for constructing internal improvements, concluding they would render life more valuable "by diminishing the stock of human misery." The letter continued to apply the ideas of the Chester *Democrat,* maintaining that "the State of New York will become, under the fostering care of intelligence and liberality, the garden of the American continent — a land in which Art shall give nature a fair play.[11]

Caldwell, a Jeffersonian to the core, and like the master prone to invent, in this case a word, started a discourse on morality by proclaiming that "the imperishable cementation . . . between the whole population of the United States" would create "a compact society" that would "be exempt from such of the poverty, wretchedness, and concomitant vice and no little of the sickliness of large cities." Caldwell was reminding European critics that their cities, by contrast, harbored the very worst excesses found on the planet, while American urban areas, with their railroads, "possess a large share of the knowledge, refinement, and polish of a city, united to the virtue and purity of the country." Railways, he claimed, promised to raise the level of national morality by bringing together the best of Jefferson's and Hamilton's worlds.[12]

Maintaining a high moral tone in a period of rapid urbanization was difficult in the face of a growing class of urban poor. Promoters rarely made explicit, however, any connection between hard times, periodic unemployment, and poverty, even though the railways' first great promotional burst extended into the 1839 national depression. When rail enthusiasts mentioned unemployment at all, they emphasized its moral effects. Perhaps they took a cue Governor Hiester of Pennsylvania gave back in 1821 when, in his annual message, he noticed that internal improvement projects in his state had hired a number of unemployed, thereby "decreasing the causes of pauperism." Pauperism did not bother the governor as much as its moral effects; "want of employment," he was sure, "produces habits of idleness, and idleness is often a fruitful source of vice."[13]

Promoters and moralists of all persuasions paid homage to the Protestant Work Ethic; all agreed that railroads were one invention calculated to cure any people of idleness. They were, in fact, the very antithesis of idle — they were ever-active instruments of a higher morality. Caldwell was certain that "man is never so liable to fall into vice, as when he is idle. Hence idleness has been denominated the mother of evil." Therefore he was sure the inverse must also be true—"the industrious and the virtuous might be pronounced identical." And, he knew that "nothing so effectually awakens and sustains the industry of a community, as a prompt and profitable market for the products of it." Solving that problem was easy: "As already demonstrated, a system of Railroads will bring every place near to a market," he promised, and "it will render industry, therefore general and vigorous."

Caldwell, like many of his generation, started with the basic assumption that railways brought wealth and comfort, which "are active sources of moral influence." Comfort, he noted, made man content, and "such a state of mind cannot fail to favor virtue. It induces men to spend their evenings, and other leisure hours, at home, in the bosoms of their families, where they are secure from vicious examples and allurements." Having argued that a device invented to move people and goods expeditiously would help keep men at home with their families and make the whole nation the better for it, he observed that "should this progressive improvement, in the condition of man, go on to millennial perfection, . . . the establishment of Rail-roads will be then looked back to, as one of the great leading causes, that have co-operated in the production of that great consummation."[14]

The anticipation of the "millennial perfection" presupposed a future populace that was not only wise, educated, virtuous, and civilized, but that also enjoyed the benefits of a healthy body and surroundings. Anyone who has perused diaries, journals, and autobiographies of nineteenth-century Americans cannot but be struck by their preoccupation with their own health and their curiosity about everyone else's. Medicine in the period was primitive. Every family could tell sad tales about loved ones who died before their biblical spans, and people did not take good health for granted. Newspapers everywhere were crammed with advertisements for patent medicines that claimed to cure everything from scalp diseases to "foot rot" and frequently offered the same elixir for both.

63

Alcohol consumption and drug usage in the nineteenth century were high because many of the medicines were little more than high-proof pain suppressors. The early railroad era was also one in which epidemics were all too common, especially yellow fever, which ranged from the deep South into the Middle Atlantic states. More vague diseases such as "ague" and "the fever" felled hardy individuals for months at a time, often attacking the men working on the railroads out in the countryside.

It was only to be expected that railway promoters would seize on the preoccupation with personal health in touting their various projects. The human body, the most common railroad metaphor of the period, may have coupled the science of communication with physical health at some level in Americans' minds. Promoters were quick to grasp the idea that railroads were metaphorical assets that strengthened the national body and on the level of physical reality promoted personal health by making it possible for everybody to avoid the debilitating diseases that lurked everywhere in the 1830s. Enthusiasts assumed any innovation that, to quote an 1829 author, gave "new vigor . . . to public industry" promoted the health of the nation, commercially, politically, and medically.[15]

The metaphoric connection between health and the national unity linked up naturally with strong public presuppositions about the basic unhealthiness of all cities. Americans have always demonstrated ambivalent attitudes towards their large urban centers. Proud of their cultural attractions, commercial prosperity, educational facilities, lively discourse, and sometimes envious of their sinful opportunities, they at the same time decried the dense concentration of people, dirt, noise, and sickness in them. The public image of cities as breeders of disease and vice contrasted with the image of rural life as offering good clean fresh air, green foliage, and vast acres of fertile land. The countryside reflected a healthy image, the city was a mixed place of opportunity, enjoyment, and pestilence — a distinction that by no means died in the twentieth century. Early railway promoters, influenced by extant images and metaphors, offered their projects to the public as investments in the common well-being. Often they were very general, for example, simply promising that their road would ensure a supply of fresh food to urban areas all year. Rarely did they make explicit their underlying assumption that a regular supply of fresh food would promote general health. They did proclaim that railroads would lower food costs dramatically and enable the poor to buy food (without discussing exactly what the impoverished were currently eating). Numerous articles dealt with the prospect of that happy day when railroads would bring fresh milk to the city to lower high infant mortality rates.

More often railway enthusiasts promoted their projects as a means of enabling people to flee the unhealthy cities. One of the earliest observers, Thomas Earle, argued in 1830 that railroads would feed cities and bring back to the farms a steady supply of fertilizer and thereby promote everyones' health. Based on a misconception that railroads would always follow the high ground, Earle proclaimed that they "will accommodate towns and villages on the sites . . . which are high and healthy, and will furnish inducements to establish towns in such places." Earle had an ingrained affinity for high ground as a synonym for good health and was dead set on placing his railroads right on top of it. He was on solid ground, for he knew that in the summer people in New Orleans regularly fled to the "highlands" of southern Mississippi; New Yorkers wandered up the Hudson; people of the Mohawk Valley climbed into the Adirondacks; and everyone who could afford it summered at a higher elevation. Railroads promised to bring down the price of escape.[16]

Caldwell took a more expansive view of railroads and health. Speaking when the Baltimore & Ohio Railroad had not even reached the Ohio River, and when any notion of a nation-wide rail system connecting North with South was met with skepticism, he confidently proclaimed that the new invention would be highly beneficial, "enabling and inducing invalids, and people of feeble constitutions, to migrate from the south to the north, in summer, and from the north to the south, in winter." Almost as if he had a crystal ball, in which he could see retirement villages in modern Florida, he continued, "thus, will those, whose infirmities and weaknesses require them, enjoy, at the proper times, the invigorating freshness of northern breezes, and the balmy mildness of the southern zephyrs."[17]

Most promoters demonstrated less fecund imaginations when claiming that railroads promoted health. Commonly they asserted that their roads would enable city people to reach nearby healthful resorts easily and comfortably. As early as 1834 promoters of the Long Island Railroad painted the attractions of summer, sand, and ocean to harried New Yorkers, claiming "the increased facilities furnished by the railroad for the enjoyment of this luxury is calculated, therefore, to subserve the health and comfort of the city, and to make the road itself a favorite and fashionable avenue." Twelve years later the desire to flee foul congestion to breathe the invigorating air of the healthful countryside had lost little of its intensity. When citizens of Philadelphia boosting the Pennsylvania Railroad published their arguments for its construction, they promised to build their road "through a country unsurpassed in variety, beauty, and grandeur of scenery, and . . . of great resort for health and pleasure." Promoters of the Long Island road and the Pennsylvania anticipated their routes would cater to the well-to-do. Up in Boston, however, the editor of the *Traveller*, a paper aptly named in this instance, applauded the designs of "the authorities on one of our roads, whose president is a thoroughly practical man," to organize "a system of cheap travelling, for the thousands in our city and outskirts who are at present, in a measure, deprived of the healthful exercise of this kind, through lack of means." The editor considered riding the trains a healthy exercise; for most people thought the idea of a day spent frolicking in the country was appealing, and as more railways were completed the sight of Sunday school picnics became commonplace. Pastors often extorted special Sunday excursion rates from companies, even as they argued the remainder of the week against running trains on the Sabbath.[18]

That the railroad helped to advance education, morality, and health was perfectly in accord with two of the promoters' larger metaphorical images — adolescence and the family. Adolescence was the normal time for instruction and growth, and rail enthusiasts effortlessly combined the various strands of imagery so that the youthful industry and nation were both seen as growing in mind and body. Similarly, moral instruction was the family's prerogative, and thus the railroad was presumed to parallel the family in binding the country together and bringing it ethical and civilizing influences. When promoters talked about education and morality and promised to uplift national standards of behavior, they meant improving the quality of the American character. They obviously be-

Promoters almost always succeeded
in associating railroads with happy images.
(Historical Pictures Service, Chicago)

lieved that their countrymen were deficient in learning and morals and that those defects were political dangers. The promoters presumed the nation's character would change, perhaps would have to change, if the country were to survive. They believed that railroads were the instruments to bring about those changes and that a higher level of knowledge was a key to their nation's future. They also assumed that if they were successful in spreading knowledge across the land, the social divisions created by class distinctions would somehow disappear.

But this is the Car of the People,
And before it shall bow all kings[1]

CHAPTER 5

Car of the People

⊢—⊢—⊢—⊢—⊢—⊢—⊢—⊢—⊢—⊢—⊢—⊢—⊢—⊢—⊢—⊣

AMERICANS had long prided themselves on building a society without artificial class distinctions, even though in Jackson's Democracy its reality often fell far short of the ideal. They avidly read foreign traveler's journals that expressed amazement at the sight of Americans of all classes commingling in enforced equality in public places and on public transportation. Conversely, Americans who traveled abroad were often struck by the formal class segregation they found. Elias H. Derby, a wealthy Massachusetts citizen, wrote in his pamphlet "Two Months Abroad" that, while on a trains to Leeds, he counted passengers and found that of the 135, 15 were traveling first class and 90 third class. But he observed that "among the latter are few of the lower orders, for in this section of England, the charges are so high, that they are debarred from rail-ways." By contrast, he pointed out that at home "our policy is not to punish travellers for their poverty, or keep females for hours standing, exposed to weather, but to give them comfortable accommodations; that, whatever may be our other failings, we treat the poor with decency and respect."[2]

Railroads, however, were the victims of a quandary of their own making; although they helped to refashion the American social structure, they were also trapped by it. Enthusiasts quickly realized that the poor and middling classes did not lobby for railway charters, raise money, locate routes, understand technology, or manage the completed roads. It took influence to wring appropriations from strapped state legislatures and city councils, while only those merchants and businessmen who had uncommitted cash reserves could afford to gamble on an untried technology. A very few railroads, most notably the Pennsylvania, attempted to democratize their ownership by sending agents door to door soliciting stock subscriptions. Afterwards its promoters argued that it was truly the road of the little man, pointing out that most stockholders owned fewer than five shares. The stock, however, sold for one hundred dollars a share, and that suggested that the railway's little man was not so small in a world where annual incomes were only three to four times as much. The fact was that the men who owned the railways or who invested the public's money in the companies were the upper crust of American society.

Most of those men believed that they were furthering the national, state, or municipal good first and foremost; they considered any personal returns in such a speculative security as lagniappe. Most early investors were surprised if their stocks paid any dividends at all — they considered that lower carrying costs, enlarged trade territory, military defense, improved mail delivery, increased land values, and national unity were reasons enough to justify sinking their means into the projects. As late as 1845 Minor spoke forcibly to this question when he observed that "we are not of those who think a railroad to be profitable must pay a large dividend. Many railroads would be profitable to a large portion of the people, if they never paid 5, or even 3 per cent."[3] Men who invested generously of their means responded to sophisticated promotional appeals that used the national unity image to its full advantage. The result, however, was that the men who owned the railways were overwhelmingly those with means and influence; whereas the people who used the railroads, from the small farmer and tinkerer to the great coastal merchants, constituted a cross section of American society.

In a nation still ambivalent about its class structure, the rail's public spokesmen were forced to respect wealth. Even while they professed they were the leading agents of a leveling movement in the country, they often appealed to class prejudices in their quest for public support. Sometimes such approaches were subtle, such as those embedded in the press descriptions of the ubiquitous general meetings that preceded the announcement of grand enterprises. Railway promoters always took great pains to publicize the fact that those who attended were highly reputable; it became standard fare to read notices in the newspapers similar to one in North Carolina that announced in 1832 "a large and respectable meeting of the citizens of Wilmington," or twelve years later another describing "the highly respectable meeting which took place at Boston [that] offers strong evidence of the estimation in which railways are held by an intelligent community." Frequently promoters equated intelligence with being well-to-do. [4]

The obvious assumption in most promotional pieces was that if the "best" elements of a community were in favor of a railroad project then others would follow their lead. Promoters occasionally made an explicit pitch to the wealthy by arguing that railways would serve only the upper crust, perpetuate the values of that class, and protect it from the mob below. One of the earliest and most forthright of these appeals was made by Caldwell, who minced no words and gave not a nod to the average man. "An elegant mode of conveyance (and such is that by Rail-road cars)," he began, "will insure the presence of elegant travelers. It will be unfashionable to appear in one of those vehicles, without being well dressed. Good breeding also will be expected and observed in them."[5]

Caldwell shared the general supposition that the presence of ladies was assumed to be proof of class. "A lady can sit in a car," he pointed out, "in as much cleanliness and comfort as in her own parlor. In each place, therefore, her wardrobe will be alike elegant," much, he contended, as was found on the very best steamboats. He then tied elegance into the morality theme so popular at the time. "But," he claimed, "external cleanliness is the native growth of purity within. . . . Hence, innocence is always arrayed in unsullied whiteness; while Guilt or Murder are wrapped in begrimed or blood-stained garments." A veteran journalist working the inaugural run of the Baltimore and Washington Railroad in 1835 shared Caldwell's sentiments but did not appear quite as interested in feminine innocence. Describing President Andrew Jackson's reception for the railroad dignitaries as one that brought everyone "unalloyed gratification," he moved quickly on to the more interesting sights and remarked happily that "the ladies presented a fair specimen of the

Obviously passengers dressed in their best finery
to ride the railroad.
(Historical Pictures Service, Chicago)

'beauty and fashion' of Baltimore; and there were not less than three hundred of them."[6]

In Boston, Caldwell showed that he had far from exhausted his ideas about railways serving the nation's better sort when he came up with his own version of Herbert Hoover's later "trickle down" theory. "Let Rail-road traveling be introduced, to the extent contemplated," he promised, "and the march of this general amelioration, in manners, refinement, and intellect, will be greatly accelerated; and that of morality will accompany it." The process he thought was simple; the cultured, mannered, and genteel would meet and mingle, and when they returned home they would impart their uplifted tone and manners to the poor souls who did not travel.[7]

Caldwell thought the rich would be attracted to railway travel by "the elegant construction and ornamental beauty of the cars." Others agreed. In March 1832 Niles inserted a notice in his newspaper that Richard Imlay had built the Frenchtown and Newcastle Railroad a new coach that "may well be called a travelling 'palace,' because of its conveniences." This may have been the first use of the term "palace car," an image hardly created to attract mechanics. Caldwell earlier asserted that opulent rolling stock "like other products of the fine arts, . . . will improve the taste of those who may travel in them." To underscore his point, he added, such luxury "substitutes higher and more refined indulgencies for lower and grosser ones."[8]

Other promoters never allowed their imaginations to soar quite as high as Caldwell's, but sympathized with his opinions about class. One "S.D." in Boston wrote the *American Railroad Journal* in 1838 that "there is one class of society for which railways may be said to be particularly made; . . . that is, the class of men of business, properly so called; that is, of men of business habits, of men of method." Although he gave a rather tortured definition of the class he was describing, S.D. had a fairly good grasp of the intellectual process by which his era was progressing toward a more open capitalism. And he was sure that "according as civilization extends, and the value of knowledge not as a means of display, but as a means of return [increases] . . . such men must increase." Minor, who had suffered through almost twenty years of reverses in promoting the

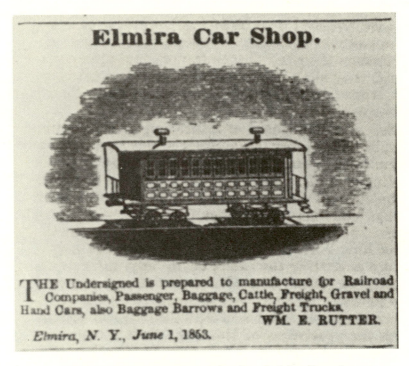

Elmira Car Shop.

THE Undersigned is prepared to manufacture for Railroad
Companies, Passenger, Baggage, Cattle, Freight, Gravel and
Hand Cars, also Baggage Barrows and Freight Trucks.

WM. E. RUTTER.

Elmira, N. Y., June 1, 1853.

Even cars built twenty years after Caldwell spoke
were less than sumptuous.
(*American Railroad Journal*, June 4, 1853)

New York and Erie Railroad agreed with S.D., arguing that "to *no place, or people,* is it of as much importance as to New York, and the businessmen of that mighty city."[9]

More frequently, however, railway promoters argued that their routes would benefit the poor as well. They appeared to be more confident when they took this tack. Equality of opportunity as a national goal was everywhere in the air and accorded very neatly with Americans' hopes for national unity. Rail advocates often walked a thin line in their public appeals, seeking to gain popular approbation for their projects without losing the financial backing of the wealthy classes. It was not an easy task, given the social flux of that period. Most enthusiasts argued that railroads would raise living standards and promote culture for all. Nary a word escaped their pens to hint that the benefits might not be equitably shared. The New York Internal Improvements convention of 1836 exposed the whole class conundrum when it argued that railroads should be built for one reason: "The railroad is the poor man's road. It is," the convention held, "the rich man's money expended for the benefit of himself and the poor man." The framers of that document saw no contradictions in their statement; just above it they had argued that such a policy "renders the State more desireable, more precious, and more esteemed in the affections of its citizens and draws forth their patriotic love." In that case, argued the promoters, the price paid by the rich was well rewarded. Minor put forth a similar argument in an 1840 editorial supporting the Harlem Railroad's right to lay its tracks in the city's streets. "Railroads," he claimed, "have justly been called *democratic* institutions, they are for the people, and rich and poor alike derive the advantages from them. In fact the benefit of the poor classes is one of our best arguments. How many laborers, living at a distance from their place of work, can, for a trifle, be transported thither, without a loss of time or strength?"[10]

A Boston and Worcester Railroad director presented another interesting argument in defense of railways for the working people in his speech at its opening festivities on July 6, 1835. Henry Williams was positively vitriolic against Boston's wealthy leaders. He started on a sour note: "The road had a sorry beginning. At first, some of our prominent men were willing to advance a few dollars to make examinations and surveys; but when called upon to take and pay for the stock, they *flinched*, and vociferously cried out '*twas madness to go on.*'" He asked the notables gathered there to consider who had actually completed the work, "Has it been done by the great men, the rich men of the times?" He was not reluctant to answer himself: "No sir! It has been accomplished by the bone and muscle of the community. By the middling interest people, by that class of men who have warm hearts, clear heads, and who possess almost a monopoly of generous public spirit." The director had reached his oratorical stride. "This class of population feel their power," he exclaimed, "they are not, and *never* can be *man-worshippers*; they do not place their trust in what are called great men, or in rich men." He went on to predict that the "common people" would build railways in the great West.[11]

Williams' remarks were those of a bitter man, quite untypical of the usual promotional literature, and yet he did not flinch from addressing the thorny question of railways and class. Neither did the 1843 "Report of the Minority on Internal Improvements Submitted to the Legislature of North Carolina," in which the members complained that their opponents denounced railways "as only calculated to benefit the rich at the expense of the poor; that their construction has occasioned a heavy loss to the State, without any adequate return; and that, consequently, they deserve not the fostering care of the public." The minority argued in rebuttal that state-aided improvements saved time and money for rich and poor alike by reducing prices, and that state funds had gone into the pockets of average North Carolinians who sold material to the railways and worked on them. This dispute was common to a number of states where taxpayers argued they incurred liabilities for an improvement that benefitted the well-to-do.[12]

A similar debate erupted seven years later in Toronto, where the working class voted against using city funds to subscribe to a local railroad project. Poor used that piece of news to unleash a diatribe against those in his own country who thought rails were the tools of the rich. He was absolutely certain that " a person who possesses the least property is in fact the most interested in railways." And he ticked off the reasons for this: "they diminish the cost of all the necessaries of life"; "they give employment where none existed before"; they "increase the rate of wages"; and "they constitute the most powerful stimulant that can be applied to business." The New York editor was willing to grant that the new invention benefitted the rich, but not, he thought, "in the same proportion nor in the same way" as it did the poor. He used a rather curious rationale to support his belief, arguing that the railway "increases the value of his [the rich man's] property, but may not add to his luxuries or comforts." That thought was open to several possible interpretations, but his flat assertion that "men are usually selfish in proportion as they are rich" and therefore "the rich never subscribe for these works so liberally in proportion to their means as those who possess only competancy or a small amount of property," was crystal clear, indeed, almost Biblical in tone.[13]

Poor was carrying on the tradition of his predecessor in the editor's chair; Minor had composed an 1844 editorial in which he maintained that railways not only served the poor, but uplifted them en masse as well. He argued that the "cause," as he kept calling it, "is doing so much to promote the prosperity, comfort, and intelligence of the millions — the mass — *the poor*! We hold that railroads are doing more than any other institution among us except our schools, towards placing the people on terms of equality, and fortunately their tendency is to level *upward*, instead of downward." He added rather weakly that railways "enable the poor man to ride as comfortably as the rich, and what is of the utmost importance to them they save more than the cost in *time*." This was one of his favorite arguments: that all the poor had to sell was their time and that, if they could save any, they thereby saved money and became more prosperous.[14]

Minor seemed obsessed by the subject, which he returned to just a month later. After a long recital of what railways did for undeveloped areas, he noted that "in no one branch of modern improvement have the calculations of theory been so variant from the results of actual experience, as in that of railroads. It was supposed," he continued, "that the advantages would be confined almost exclusively to the commercial, the travelling, and the non-productive classes of the community; and that farmers and mechanics, the laboring and producing classes, would derive very little benefit from them." Writing in the midst of the worst depression the nation had experienced, he promised "it is the railroad that places all on the level, that revives and stimulates industry, that furnishes facilities and encouragement to labor and production, and distributes and equalizes, within the sphere of its influence, their advantages and profits." It was a more sophisticated variant on the "equal rights for all, special privileges for none" battle cry.[15]

In the midst of the acrimonious debates in 1845 over the admission of Texas to the Union, Minor returned to his theme of serving the poor and tied it in very nicely into the predominant national unity image. Once again he asserted that "the process of *levelling* is *upward*," but this time he was a little more specific in describing it. "Railroads tend to elevate," he began, "to extend and increase *knowledge* as well as business; and in *our* country especially, they will unite us more closely as a people, and bind us together as a common brotherhood, unless those demons, *indolence and ambition* . . . sap the foundations of the republic by fostering sectional prejudices, and thus plunge us into anarchy, bloodshed, and ruin." Minor agreed wholeheartedly with the Chevalier de Gerstner, who was reported by the Savannah *Georgian* in 1841 to have called railroads "popular democratic establishments." And indeed, as much as he might have disputed it, the New York editor also was in accord with Caldwell in assuming that rails would create a culture that would uplift and unite all Americans of whatever class.[16]

On a more basic level, railways were sometimes adjudged a direct, practical help for the poor, as in 1842 when the *Miners' Journal* covered the opening ceremonies of the Pottsville and Philadelphia Railroad. After reciting all the usual anticipated gains, the *Journal* noted that the road would carry great quantities of coal to the Quaker City thereby lowering the fuel's cost, which meant that "'a hard winter for the poor' will lose a part at least of its painful significance." Four years later the *American Railroad Journal* ran a long piece commenting on a story taken from the Macon *Messenger* that described how a certain Judge Tarver in Jefferson County, Georgia, was distraught that many of his neighbors were starving because of poor crops. With his own money Tarver bought 1,150 bushels of corn and 10 hogsheads of bacon in Savannah that "he distributed among them at moderate prices on credit." Lauding Tarver's philanthropy, Minor boasted "that this is one of the

Minor thought a typical passenger car of the 1840s,
such as this one advertising a braking system,
was a leveling innovation.
(*American Railroad Journal*)

benefits derived from railroads. The Central's road being able to lay down the provisions, at a very low rate, near the judge's residence."[17]

Railroad promoters were prescient to have foreseen their projects' wider ramifications; they understood that their roads would bring large-scale social changes in their wake. Most importantly, they were willing to popularize the notion that railways had important contributions to make to America, aside from their commercial benefits. In many respects, theirs were precapitalist arguments. They looked at the welfare of the larger public and emphasized, not the potentialities for private gain from the railways, but rather what their construction would do for the body politic. Enthusiasts promised that their projects would go far to narrow the social and income gaps that tended to pit American against American. Their vision of the new nation was not one where the upper classes were dragged down in the name of some ideological presumption, but rather one in which the lower orders would be raised. Minor understood these expectations when he announced in 1845 that "the spirit of the age is onward."[18] What he meant, of course, was that it was ever upward towards an increased measure of prosperity on every social level. And he instinctively knew that a nation with a growing disdain for anything that smacked of inherited rank, whose citizens shared equitably in its overall material success and comforts, was one unlikely to tear asunder or to fade quietly into the pages of history. Certainly not one with railways and so much available land.

CHAPTER 6

Wealth of Lands

├─┼─┼─┼─┼─┼─┼─┼─┼─┼─┼─┼─┼─┼─┼─┼─┤

RAILWAY promoters' assurances that their projects would raise land values permeated the literature of the first two railroad decades. Enthusiasts everywhere understood that land was a central element in any definition of the American character. In a nation as overwhelmingly rural as the United States, class, status, and political preferment rested primarily upon the ownership of land; important social gradations depended upon the size, location, and value of the fields. Advocates forcefully argued that their railways would improve everyone's estate and that even the landless would benefit from their construction.

Land was a powerful symbol that carried only positive metaphorical overtones. As the promoters used it, land represented prosperity or, more importantly, the promise of wealth to come. Land was the most valuable asset in the United States, and railway publicists promised their roads would increase the total value of the country's real estate and thereby its national wealth. Their more direct appeal, however, was the promise of higher estate values for any landowner. Thus, the argument for land development intertwined personal and national prosperity; pursuit of private interests in the guise of railways would redound to the common welfare.

By the 1840s, promoters and railway financiers discovered that isolated lands had a pecuniary worth that they could extract even before their railroads gave them any market value. Advocates successfully petitioned local, state, and federal officials to grant land to unbuilt railroads so that company officials could transform its potential value into real dollars to pay construction costs. The financing technique fit perfectly with that aspect of the nation's character that held there was an intimate relationship between the health of the individual and that of his country. The republic's common fund, tapped for the betterment of the few, would ensure the prosperity of all. The national unity image worked in both directions.

Land, as a symbol, appealed on several levels. Land was one of democracy's basic elements, especially in a nation with millions of undistributed acres. From the nation's founding, legislators had labored to make state and federal lands available at nominal prices that would encourage the spread of a rural democracy across the continent. Railways promised to aid that distribution by opening up great areas for settlement to enable land sales to keep pace with the rapid population growth. Moreover, if there was a correlation between wealth and literacy railroads would, by raising land values, be increasing the size of the enlightened free citizenry and helping to ameliorate class differences. Few enthusiasts, however, felt they had to explain that a rural citizenry in easy communication with urban areas, enjoying high levels of personal wealth, and freely partaking in the political process, would everywhere uplift the nation's morals.

More frequently promoters cited the connection between higher land values and a more secure national unity. Their assurances that the value of land would rise carried the explicit promise that greater geographical, political, and class unity would ensue. Good, free land was still available in parts of the East and in greater quantities in the South and West. The idea of the nation's finding a common cause in building railways to make this acreage available to the landless and the small farmers was a powerful unifying force. A nation of free farmers settled in all the country's major sections, yet linked to local and regional markets by rail, promoters believed, would go far toward cementing the Union. And implicit in their promotion of land development was their faith in the idea that common occupational outlooks and financial levels would lead to political similarities everywhere.

The importance of land as a symbol meshed neatly with the realities promoters faced. They had to raise the bulk of their funds from eastern urban interests in a country where over three-quarters of its citizens earned their incomes directly from the land. Moreover, railway publicists could not forget that in every state legislature, the so-called "country interests" controlled the majority of the votes and determined how the public's funds were spent. To appeal to the self-interest of both urban and rural constituencies, promoters argued their schemes in the name of the national good, using sophisticated, often metaphorical arguments, illustrating the vital relationships between land and the nation's welfare.

Promoters began to dangle the lure of instant wealth from sharply increased real-estate prices before the public as early as the canal era and stepped up the frequency and variety of their arguments during the following decades of the railway boom. Their first messages were the essence of simplicity, sometimes little more than passing mentions of the subject, taking for granted that everyone in a country of farmers thoroughly understood that *any* transportation would raise the value of their fields. Governor Hiester of Pennsylvania, for example, in his 1822 annual message assumed that he need say no more than that an extensive system of state works would reduce transport costs while "increasing the value of lands, and enabling many who were hitherto destitute of the opportunity, now to reach a market with the production of their industry." Directly north of the Keystone state, De Witt Clinton, in a report on his survey for a railroad from Portage Summit, Ohio, to the Hudson River in 1832, mentioned that railways "increase the value of lands" and also "the fruits of the earth in more remote situations." Six years earlier Governor Shulze of Pennsylvania conjured up a not very edifying metaphor when he contended that internal improvements would give "a value to what would otherwise have rotted on the surface, or lain neglected in the bowels of the earth." Moreover, he continued, an improvement "raises the price of land" and gives the remote farmers' crops a market value.[1]

Everybody agreed that canals and railways would increase the value of nearby lands, but nobody seemed to know by how much. Long after the canals and railways were constructed, the rule of thumb appeared to be that the longer promoters argued the point the more land appreciated. The arguments, or more accurately, the boasts, guesses, and outright lies, started as early as 1824, when the commissioners for promoting internal improvements in Pennsylvania quoted a resident of western New York who swore that along the Erie Canal, "land experienced a rise equal to an average of $5 an acre, in one year; produce doubled in price, and cash is given for everything that we have for sale." Earlier the same commissioners had reported that, with a new canal in New Hampshire, "the wood-land there has risen in price . . . from 2 dollars to 6, 8 and 10 dollars per acre." Although they weakened their arguments by not mentioning earlier land prices, probably on the assumption that their contemporaries knew what unimproved land prices were, the quoted figures were still impressively high.[2]

An anonymous writer to the *North American Review* in 1829 was one of the earliest to take the valuation pitch one giant step farther. His immediate purpose was to publicize the need for a railroad from Boston to the Hudson River; after pointing out the money this state-built route would pour into Massachusetts' coffers, he cited the advantages "in the increase of business, and the increased value of property in the state." All that was part of the standard literature. He continued to admit that he could offer no idea of the precise value of such benefits, but he thought that "the immediate increase of the value of real estate in the Commonwealth would be more than equal to the whole cost of the road." Here he hit upon an idea that many promoters later picked up, for he was saying that, for accounting purposes, the railroad would be free! Actually it was even better than that; he estimated "the cost will be twice repaid, once in refunding that cost in the direct income of the road, and once in other pecuniary benefits which the citizens of the Commonwealth will derive from it."[3]

Once the appealing idea that railroads would increase land values enough to cover the actual cost of the improvement had been planted in promoters' minds, it did not take them long to make the next logical move and argue that the rise in land values would no doubt exceed the railway's cost. William Jackson explained all this to the Charitable Mechanic Association in Boston in 1829, when he told the assemblage that if the construction of a railroad from that city were undertaken "the increased value of property, in Boston only, will be much more than sufficient to defray the whole expense of this road." He was just beginning, however; he riveted their attention when he hypothesized that if property in that city was assessed at about 70 million dollars, and its value rose only 6 or 8 percent, that "would amount to a sum nearly sufficient to construct a Rail Road, with a double track to Albany." But, he warned his listeners, if the improvement were not built, the value of their property would fall as their city fell farther behind New York in the race for western trade. In that case, the railroad's increase in their property values was much higher, for they could assume their values would fall in the road's absence.[4]

Southerners could make like arguments with equal facility. In Virginia, a civil engineer speaking in 1833 on behalf of the Petersburgh Railroad asserted without qualification that "the value of property, within five miles of the road, has increased already *more than the road has cost*; and we hesitate not to say that the increased value for five years to come will be greater than for the same period past." Even farther South, the editor of the Savannah *Georgian*, an avid supporter of internal improvements, told his readers in 1841, "we doubt whether a railroad can be found in the world which has not increased the value of the land, throughout the entire extent; in some cases one, two, three hundred per cent." Eight years later the Baltimore *American* was certain the latter estimate was nearer the mark. The editor assured his readers that "if the Baltimore and Ohio Railroad were now finished, there is little question that the enhanced value of property along the line, would be "three times the cost of the Road." To support his contention, he ran a copy of a letter from the Nashville and Chattanooga Railroad's president, who explained that lots in Nashville had risen, thanks to the railway, three hundred dollars per acre, while plots three to ninety miles out of the town had appreciated anywhere from five dollars to fifteen dollars per acre. He also thought the lands lying ten miles on each side of the track had increased in value more than three times the whole cost of his road.[5]

Promoters understood that land values did not always rise equally along a road. They wrestled with that problem for years because often people opposed their projects on the grounds that they would aid some areas and not others, or that a particular city would benefit to a greater degree than the surrounding countryside. Railway supporters usually responded that their projects would benefit everyone to some degree, while admitting that some folks would undoubtedly gain more than others. Occasionally they could even admit some landowners would lose. In 1830 the Pennsylvania legislature's Committee on Inland Navigation appealed to the "country set," as it sought a state-wide consensus to raise additional taxes to complete the state works. In its report, the committee arrived at the surprising conclusion that "the canals leading to the cities of New-York and Philadelphia, have uniformly diminished the value of land near those cities, and enhanced it at a distance." That body did not give the slightest hint as to how it arrived at this conclusion, but it may be inferred that the farmers immediately adjacent to those cities, who had long enjoyed a monopoly of the nearby produce markets, lost their advantage to lands further out along the canals and their land values declined proportionately.[6]

A year later in 1831, when "A Pennsylvanian" wrote a pamphlet supporting the continuation of the state works, he developed a very sophisticated method for estimating the increase in real-estate prices along them. He started with the eye-opening assertion that all other transportation benefits fade into insignificance "when compared with the permanent enhancement of the value of the lands of the state, of which no small part are raised in price from 50 to 500 per cent." In case his readers missed his point, he inserted a footnote explaining that the increase in the value of land in Schuylkill county and "its neighbourhood alone" was equal to the whole cost of the state works. He then reprinted, without attribution, a report arguing for a circular theory of land values that was remarkably similar to Walter Christaller's twentieth-century locational theories, in which the unknown author drew five concentric circles around Pittsburgh, each thirty miles farther out. He calculated that acreage within the smallest circle had appreciated due to the state works an average of $2.50 per acre and did the same calculation for each ring out to the fifth, where acreage had risen only 50 cents. Knowing the areas of the circles, he totaled the increases and found they reached over 68 million dollars. Even if wildly in error, it was a convincing exercise supporting the logical premise that the farther land was from an improvement, the less it was worth.[7]

Numerous articles claiming ever-larger real-estate gains prompted

Poor to remark in his *Journal* that railroads' great advantages are "not measured so much by the dividends they pay, as by the enhanced value they give to the property of the sections through which they run, and in the town in which they terminate." He pointed out that since nearly everyone owned property, all had a vital interest in internal improvements, folding the whole discussion nicely into the national unity image, even if he did overstate the extent of land ownership. A scant two months later Poor printed an article he took from the Springfield, Illinois, *Journal*, in which that midwestern editor agreed the "railroad will double, yea triple the value of farms in our portion of the state." Carried away by his enthusiasm for the coming real-estate boom, the newspaperman extended the promoters' arguments to absurdity when he suggested that "farmers would make money in giving away half their landed property to secure their construction."[8]

Promoters came up with many variants on the argument that railroad development increased land value. One originated only six months after navvies began construction of the Baltimore and Ohio Railroad in 1828. William Jackson, speaking on a cold January evening, threatened that if Boston were left behind in the race for the western trade the town would grow poorer and all property values would fall. "No axiom is more certain," he assured his audience, "than that capital will go where it can find the most profitable employment, and it is equally certain to a great extent, that it will carry its owners with it." Jackson had a clear image of capitalists: they were "the most enterprising, who are now contributing most to the prosperity of your city," and he promised that if they left, presumably for a railroad town, "in ten years from this time, there will be a diminution in the value of property in this city to an amount more, much more, than sufficient to construct this road." Even negative values of railroads were fully equal to the cost of their construction.[9]

The intimate relationship between land value and population growth was a powerful potion in the southern states where, by the 1830 census, readers were well aware that they were falling behind in attracting newcomers and paying a political penalty as a result. Many Dixie promoters promised their railways would remedy that evil. The Frederick, Maryland, *Herald* in 1831, for example, tackled this subject in an editorial that pointed out the beneficent results felt there even before the railroad arrived. The editor proudly announced a "rapid increase of our population, and a correspondent rise in rents." And the future looked even rosier since "we hear almost daily of capitalists who intend to open stores." But the real boon for the town, he thought, was the fact that "the great flour market of the state will concentrate in Frederick; and as a consequence the population will increase with great rapidity." When news of another Dominion project, the Portsmouth and Roanoke Railroad, reached New York in 1834, Minor promoted its construction in his paper, arguing in part that railroads in Virginia and North Carolina "will have the tendency to check immigration, and of course to reestablish a different and more gratifying state of things in those States." The out-migration from the region would be stemmed, he thought, because the railroads would insure that "lands which have for years been of no value, or of so little value as to remain uncultivated, will again be brought into use." The Richmond *Enquirer* published portions of a speech given in the house of delegates in which a lawmaker berated his colleagues for not supporting internal improvements, charging that if they had, "the real and personal property of Virgina would have been worth 200 millions more than it is, and her population 300,000 *freemen* more."[10]

Southerners were not the only ones to worry about population growth; along with real estate valuations it was rapidly becoming an important denominator of prosperity and progress. When a Philadelphia citizens' committee presented its petition in behalf of the Pennsylvania Railroad to their townsfolk, it was careful to point out "it is obvious . . . that the value of property throughout the Commonwealth, and the population will be increased to an extent which at present, it might not be prudent to predict."[11]

The Philadelphia committee was hesitant to predict the widespread ramifications of rising real-estate values, but many promoters were not. Everywhere they looked they saw pleasing consequences attractive to potential supporters. Some, like the Frederick editor, envisioned rising rents bringing higher profits to local capitalists. Others allowed their imaginations to wander farther afield. A Mr. Dexter, an engineer on the South Carolina Railroad, was convinced that higher property values would "arrest the evils which the mode of cultivating the soil at the South has brought upon them."[12]

Minor cut out a newspaper article in 1844 that reported some thoughtful official on the "Southern Railroad of Michigan," probably later the Michigan Southern, who reasoned that if land values rose in some proportion to the railway's value, he should be able to use that increase to pay for construction. He toyed with the idea of paying for labor with land warrants which, he explained, "being the same as cash to those who use them for the purchase of public land, a great many are induced to seek employment on the road for the purpose of applying the proceeds of their labor, [to] obtaining the land." If it worked as he claimed, the idea was brilliant, enabling the company in the middle of a great depression to build its road on credit, knowing its workers would take up nearby lands and become the line's future customers. Moreover, the scheme saved money because, as the official admitted, the warrants were worth less than cash, although the workers would recoup their losses through the value added to their lands once the railway passed through. He forgot to mention that the warrants saved his company the cost of buying capital to pay wages.[13]

The land-warrant arrangement was a precursor of later attempts to persuade state and federal governments to grant free lands to railway companies. The idea of using public lands to finance private railroads became popular in the 1840s, when the nation suffered from a severe shortage of venture capital. The logic of the proposal impressed almost everyone. Unimproved public lands had only that value which governments settled on them, produced nothing of importance, and actually cost civil authorities money to survey and hold them. If lands were granted to the companies, sold off to farmers, and their proceeds used to spike rails through the lands, their value would appreciate, the tax bases would increase, agricultural production would rise, and civilization would push the wilderness back a little farther; the entire nation would be that much more valuable. Minor, who had come out in his pages in the early 1840s against any more state aid to railroads, enthusiastically picked up the idea of using public lands in lieu of money when, in 1847, he supported a bill before Congress proposing to appropriate public lands to projects to "facilitate the transportation of mail." A year

When the railroad came to Athens, Georgia, in the 1840s,
it brought increased prosperity and activity.
The passengers at the end of the track look
as if they had arrived at the promised land.
(University of Georgia Libraries)

later he applauded the Illinois state legislature for giving generous land grants to railroads within the state.[14]

As railways opened up millions of acres of public lands, they also brought forth increased agricultural production. Early promoters had forseen that their railroads would encourage larger crops, but in their wildest dreams they could not have guessed the extent to which it would happen. In 1835 Samuel D. Ingham, president of the Beaver Meadow Railroad and Coal Company, an incongruous name for an industrial enterprise, predicted that improved transportation would "give value to property in the adjoining country," and would, as he quaintly put it, give "a stimulus to its enterprise." A southern newspaper editor worked the idea a little more and concluded that "the railroad has completely revolutionized the country, converted its waste places into smiling villages, made the hitherto uncultivated districts, swell with the labor of industry, and the harvest of the husbandman." Poor agreed when he predicted in 1849 that the great "net" of railways spreading West "will not only in many cases double the value [of land], but it will infinitely increase the amount of agricultural productions." While everyone accepted the idea that agricultural output would rise as property values increased, nobody ever discussed the exact connection between the two. It became simply a truth. When the president of the New Albany and Salem Railroad was in New York raising money for his line in 1849, for example, he pointed out that "not only will the stock yield handsome dividends, but every acre of land will be enhanced in value, every kind of produce will command higher prices, and every department of business will be promoted." Earlier promoters promised that railroads would bring subsistence farms into the cash economy, thereby increasing the value and prices of the farmers' crops. At the same time they promised that food costs in metropolitan areas would decline after railways were completed.[15]

The promise of enhanced land values was a powerful inducement for Americans everywhere to support railroad construction. And the promoters' arguments promised something for everyone. Land owners would profit from their holdings' appreciation; farmers could look forward to rising incomes and falling transport costs; urbanites could savor fresh produce at all seasons and enjoy a greater variety of consumables, better health, cheaper food, larger profits

MR. H. R. CAMPBELL'S LOCOMOTIVE ENGINE.

The locomotives of Campbell's 4-4-0 wheel arrangement
were the workhorses that hauled the crops
out of newly opened regions.
Note the outside frame on the engine.
(*American Railroad Journal*)

from rental properties, better city services, population increases, broader markets, and dependable communications with the outside world. Best of all, increased real-estate appraisals would more than cover the building costs. The counties, villages, and cities located along proposed routes that pledged tax dollars to the railways' stock could retire their debts from the increased land valuations, while municipal authorities would receive public services. It was a beautifully compact set of enticements that appealed to almost every constituency.

But most of all, the promoters were appealing to a deeply ingrained American image embedded in a belief in the primacy of land and of the men who owned and worked it. Land was the great national treasure, and promoters' promises to give remote lands value, real value, for the first time, to enable enterprising individuals to reap the mineral, timber, and crop harvests for their own good and for the welfare of the nation were simply practical steps towards strengthening national unity.

CHAPTER 7

This Land of Promise

├──┼──┼──┼──┼──┼──┼──┼──┼──┼──┼──┼──┼──┼──┼──┤

RAILROAD promoters recognized that the American character was compounded of equal elements of deep-seated fear and overweening pride. They probed the admixture, soothing their countrymen's worst anxieties and exploiting the national character's more positive aspects, which often lay much closer to the surface, especially its proclivity to expect a rosier future. Nowhere was this appeal to native optimism more evident than in the literature that touched on the possibility that railroads would unlock the treasures of the West.

Nothing so captured Americans' imaginations as their West. It became a metaphor for the character of America. For generations, it stood as the quintessential symbol for everything that made the country unique. The adjectives that promoters used to describe the West were those that were often applied to the entire nation. Enthusiasts loved to emphasize that the West was big, continental in scope, and, like the nation itself, boundless, with its limits always beyond the horizon. Writers emphasized the West's fertility, evoking a natural comparison with the whole nation's tremendous population growth, scientific maturity, and ability to generate new ideas. Americans were also convinced their West was a great national storehouse. The undeveloped region was like money in the U.S. bank account to be drawn upon to replenish operating capital from time to time. Above all, the West was there to serve the national good; it was owned by all and it was an important goal in a nation many feared was tearing itself apart. It was more amorphous than most goals, but it gave promoters a handy geographical destination for their roads. They were going to tap the West's riches; the number of railroad companies with "and Western" in their corporate names was ample testimony to that belief.

Interestingly, the language promoters used to describe the West bore striking similarities to that they used to characterize the railroads themselves. Like the wilderness, railroads were great, continental, fertile in that they spawned countless imitators and supporting businesses, keys to prosperity, servants of the nation's good, and, for many, goals. Railways, too, were celebrations of the country's good fortune and wisdom. They were the right application of new scientific principles to America's endless natural resources that would help it to overcome its profound defects. Railroads and the West naturally joined together metaphorically and otherwise to illustrate the character of the nation.

The railway advocates' early "Wests" were located anywhere not many people lived, northern Vermont, upstate New York, the southern tier of the Empire state, northwest Pennsylvania, everywhere in the South, west of the Appalachians, and out in the boondocks of Ohio, Indiana, Illinois, and Michigan. As railways pushed up to the edges of these wildernesses, however, a subtle redefinition of what constituted a West occurred. Wests could have people, villages, towns, post offices, roads, taverns, and even newspapers and still be Wests. Once railroads, as the agents of progress and modernity intruded, however, the areas immediately became something other than Wests. And this made logical sense. If railroads transformed already mature regions and were a vital part of Americans' image of an advanced civilization, then their effect on any West could only be explosive. These notions, widespread by the mid-1830s, left ample room for Wests in the East to coexist with the image of the Great West that lay out across the mighty Mississippi.

As befitted a practical lot of men, however, railroad enthusiasts were not interested in defining a West; their Wests were more in the order of a goal, places to reach out to, Edens to be tightly bound to the rest of the nation with bands of iron for the benefit of all, as they liked to say. But as children of the Romantic Age and agents of a Manifest Destiny, railway promoters could not help taking on the coloration of their times when describing what they expected to find "out there." Witness the editor of the *Knickerbocker* who, as early as 1837, predicted a transcontinental railroad. When he gazed west he saw "the mountains of coal, the vast meadow seas, the fields of salt, the mighty forests, with their trees two hundred and fifty feet in height, the stores of magnesia, the crystallized lakes of valuable salts." Others, schooled in the classical tradition, identified the West with antiquity. Thomas Hart Benton, senator from Missouri and father-in-law of "The Pathfinder," General John C. Fremont, habitually spoke of the West as "rich like Egypt." The lesser-known William G. Moorhead, president of the Sunbury and Erie Rail Road, announced to his stockholders in 1859 that the wealth of more than fourteen thousand square miles of our [Pennsylvania's] territory, awaits in the silence almost of an Arabian desert, a highway to the markets of the world." The editor of the Savannah *Georgian* raised his metaphorical sights a bit higher when he rhapsodized that "it is pleasant, sometimes, to send our thoughts in advance of the times," to the West, where Americans could "like the spies of old, revel in the land of promise, and bring back from it those rich fruits and those good reports, which shall stimulate us to go forward and enter upon their possession."[1]

Where some saw magnesia, of all things, and others saw fruits, all agreed that the West was surely the garden of the world. Minor, in an 1835 editorial, was more direct about it all; it was almost as if those bearing the responsibility for introducing modern science to the romantic age had the responsibility to couch it in less flowery rhetoric. "The territory between the Lakes, the Ohio River, and the Rocky Mountains," was, he assured his readers, simply "the garden of the world." Ten months after he used the same metaphor in behalf of his Erie Railroad, promising that it "will open another ready avenue to the fertile valleys of the garden of the world." The Chicago *Advertiser* some eighteen years later in 1853 showed the timelessness of apt metaphors when the editor used it to push for construction of a road from Chicago to St. Louis. After the usual bunkum assuring everyone that the line would be "one of the most productive roads in the Union," the editor "proved" it by reporting that "the country through which this road passes has been called by all geographers and journalists who traveled over it, the garden spot of the state, and of the West." Those of a practical bent recognized the contradiction inherent in the wilderness-garden image. Thomas Fernon, president of the North Pennsylvania Railroad certainly did; despite his zeal to promote his road as Philadelphia's great north route to western New York, he could not quite bring himself to use the garden-spot metaphor to describe the countryside it would open up. He was a bit more realistic, describing it as "a wilderness, awaiting the axe and the plough."[2]

A year earlier Poor had taken the same prosaic thought and wrapped it in a more romantic mantle when he noted that "we are a country of boundless resources" and "it must be remembered that we are reclaiming a continent from a state of nature." Poor was always wont to look at everything in larger terms, and the West offered a tempting target. Soon he took aim again in an article ostensibly on Chicago's explosive growth. He was more anxious, however, to point out that "during the same period, a vast territory, embracing an area equal to that of several of our largest States, will have been reclaimed from nature, and filled with an active, industrious and prosperous people. Where," he asked rhetorically, "can the world show a parallell [*sic*]?"[3]

Poor was playing with one of the most common images of the West — its greatness. "Great" was an integral, if often unstated, element of every western metaphor, and most writers used the adjective without explanation or definition. Thus, a Danville and Pottsville Rail Road Company committee report for 1839 declared that its road "will keep open at all seasons of the year a direct and speedy communication with the great west." A Pennsylvania state legislature committee capitalized on the notion in 1845 when it reported that New York, Pennsylvania, Maryland, and Virginia have "been expending millions of money to secure . . . the immense trade of the 'Great West.'" And Roebling played down railroad competition with the observance that "we will remember the Great West offers room for us all!" When Poor looked over his railroad map at mid-century, he concluded that the network of rails creeping across Ohio demonstrated that "the great west with all her resources and productions will be opened to the world. Eastern arithmetic," he added, "has no rule by which to compute the extent of trade from this course."[4]

Some railway promoters looked at the West and saw nothing except vast areas and distant horizons almost too large to do justice to with mere words. The West was sometimes overwhelming. A writer in the *American Railroad Journal* in 1845 thought so, observing that "the boundless and fertile west will furnish an amount of produce, almost beyond ordinary comprehension." Minor was not immune to the image of the West as limitless either. A month later when he lectured his readers on the absolute necessity for eastern cities, especially New York, to hold the western trade, he promised "a city sustained by that trade can never languish, for the increase of production of the western states is almost boundless." Eli Bowen, author of *The Pictorial Sketchbook of Pennsylvania* (1852) and noted for his *U.S. Post-Office Guide*, was so taken with the West, in his case the northwestern portion of his native state, that he almost ran out of adjectives to describe its extent. His Sunbury and Erie Railroad, if ever built, he claimed would traverse land that "is rich in every source of intrinsic wealth; vast quantities of timber of the best kind for building or shipping purposes, as well as an inexhaustible supply of anthracite and bituminous coals and iron ore, together with the produce of a rich farming district, will seek a market over this road." Later he characterized the wilderness as the repository of "an incalculable amount of wealth." Bowen's West had no beginnings or ends, no limits at all, like his United States.[5]

Americans were only about a half century removed from British ownership, so it was only natural that their own vast, remote provinces should remind them of a colonial appendage. The empire metaphor popped up as early as 1827, when the citizens of Baltimore met and concluded that "when we regard the situation of Baltimore, as respects the populous and productive empire growing up in her rear," only a railway could secure "the larger portion of the western trade." The officers of the Louisville, Cincinnati and Charleston Railroad Company adopted the same metaphor in their 1840 annual report and grafted it to the image of the West as youthful Eastern cities, the officials explained, "gather strength from the contributions of that mighty empire west, which like a giant, has sprung from its cradle." The empire metaphor was popular in the

South, too, as the editor of the Macon *Messenger* illustrated when he suggested in 1851 that his readers "lose no time in extending their business relations to East Tennessee. She is a young Empire in herself."[6] He could have added that East Tennessee was also a West. An empire, of course, suggested an organization to facilitate large-scale trade, an idea that blended nicely with already preconceived notions of the West's usefulness. The whole idea of a captive trading region, implicit in the earliest railway literature, became more fixed as the years followed and as roads actually created commercial empires beholden to them. As railroad competition dramatically increased in the 1850s, the empire metaphor took on a more clearly delineated meaning; it became commercial in nature and reflected a new image.

That metaphorical redefinition lay in the future, however; at the railroads' birth, their enthusiasts fell easily into a metaphor that emphasized fertility, the potential richness that lay locked in the untapped western regions. *DeBow's Review* reprinted a report Colonel Gadsden of South Carolina submitted to the 1845 Memphis railroad convention. There Gadsden contrasted the specter of mass starvation that he thought kept "the European countries in an annual state of alarm" with the Mississippi Valley from which he was sure "the deficiencies of other portions of the world can be supplied from the overflowing granaries of this land of promise."[7]

Railroad publicists did not originate the fertility metaphor; it had been a vital element in American literature since Jamestown. Promoters, however, continued the metaphor and gave it new meanings and directions. To some, fertility indicated potential wealth and ultimately progress. Those citizens who agitated for a Baltimore railroad in 1827 opened their petition with the modest assertion that "the fertile districts lying west of the Allegheny ridge, and watered by the Ohio and the Mississippi, are among the most remarkable in the world." But the drafters of that document continued with a slightly different twist when they claimed that "there are countries, perhaps, which excel a part of the regions we speak of, in fertility, and in the value of their products; but none whose progress is to be compared to theirs." The rate of progress in exploiting the West's natural fertility was more important than its output.[8]

Indeed, easterners constantly marveled at western growth rates, proof, many said, of the immense benefits that resulted from better transportation. Minor noted this phenomenon in 1835, after the Buckeye state opened the Ohio and Miami canals. "The brief statement appended," he promised, "shows conclusively the immense increase of business in the *West.*" A Macon editor added the fertility metaphor to his exhortation to fellow Georgians to tap the East Tennessee trade. He painted a rosy picture of "her rich valleys and fertile hill sides [that] are destined to teem with valuable products." Chicago promoters resorted to the same metaphor when, in 1853, the local *Advocate* praised its territory to the south as the "most fertile and beautiful country in the world." The editor pointed out, however, that "with its unsurpassed agricultural, manufacturing, and mineral advantages, and the salubrity of the climate, as soon as they are seen and known, will invite a flood of immigration of the best character to improve every acre of land convenient" to the proposed railroad. Fertility was potential, simply awaiting railroads and immigrants to release the West's pent-up treasures.[9]

A Mr. Parry, a member of the New Jersey legislature, made this point in an 1854 debate over the South Jersey Central and Air Line Railroad bill, when he pointed out to his fellow congressmen that "the unparallelled [*sic*] prosperity of the Western States is owing more to the construction of railroads through their midst than to any other artificial cause." His metaphor took firm root in its own rich soil as he rhetorically asked, "to what would the great fertility of their soil amount, if they had not the means of carrying its products speedily to market?" Without citing his sources, Parry told his colleagues that "a comparison of the wealth of the counties having railroads with other parts of the states, shows that their greatest prosperity is along the railroad lines," and he was sure that "the hardy pioneers of the west, as soon as they get their land cleared, want a railroad to carry their crops to market, being well persuaded that a market will not come to them."[10]

The fertility metaphor not only hinted at future potential and the common good, but also implied wealth and richness. DeBow illustrated this very nicely when he extracted a long quote from *Hunt's Merchant's Magazine* in 1846 that began, "the West is richer than the East in the surplus products of the soil, and every year will increase its advantage." The author guessed that "the West, in sixty years, will probably contain *one hundred millions* of people, while the East will have but twenty millions." His West, like that of many other commentators, was always in a state of becoming—like railroads. And its potential was unlimited. President Patterson of the Pennsylvania Railroad summed it up succinctly in his 1852 annual report when he told his stockholders that "we may confidently anticipate the rich harvest which awaits its [the Pennsylvania's] completion." He knew who would benefit from that "harvest." "It is right to speak of *revenue* to the stockholders," he counseled, "as *secondary* to the GREAT PUBLIC BENEFIT, which it was the primary object of this work to secure."[11]

People and transportation were the only missing ingredients needed to open the rich harvest locked in the nation's West. Railway promoters understood that simply describing the West's vast riches was not sufficient to lure capital and folks into the wilderness. Minor noted this in 1837 when he pointed out that "if natural advantages, such as those of location, climate, &c. are to be solely relied upon, the Indians on the Pacific might indulge a reasonable hope of obtaining and holding to our exclusion, the whole China and Pacific trade."[12]

These new pockets of civilization were destined to get rich quickly, or so most Americans chose to believe. This idea was so common it even took root in rural Tennessee, where the editor of the Trenton *Emporium* noted that "the valley of the Mississippi is destined not only to sustain its countless millions of future population, but . . . to become the granary and storehouse of a large portion of the civilized world." At mid-century Poor noticed that the great emigration into the West was drawing off population from the East and that the emigrants were eventually sending manufactured goods and foodstuffs back to the seaboard. The newly resettled people, Poor thought, "have shortened the agricultural age of the Ohio Valley to a period measured by tens instead of hundreds of years. They are now bringing us the products of Pittsburgh, Wheeling, and Cincinnati workshops." The New York editor even had an eye for the insignificant but telling anecdote; he commented that "Nashville bids highest for our professors."[13]

Even the most illiberal and parochial advocates could lift their eyes above their local concerns and envision products of the prolific West clogging the rail arteries leading to all the Atlantic port cities. Congressman Richard M. Johnson of Kentucky, an original War Hawk back in 1812 and soon to become vice president under Martin Van Buren, used this appeal to the House of Representatives in 1835 to argue that the federal government should purchase stock in the Louisville and Portland Canal. He cited endless examples of federal funds spent on improvements elsewhere in the country and contrasted them with how little had been spent in the West. Then he made his telling point: "The commerce of the west has been greatly underrated," he claimed, because "our progress has been so rapid that the imagination was startled at the reality." The size of the trade pouring out of the West had already exceeded the earlier overblown metaphorical conceptions of that bounty. Real events out there were outrunning the ability of eastern imaginations to conceptualize them.[14]

The happiest aspect of the wilderness's expected cornucopia was that every place would enjoy unparalleled benefits. Railway promoters called for their cities or states to build roads simply to maintain their relative commercial standings, but with all that potential lying out there they had little interest in capturing a rival's trading territory. That strategy became popular only after the eastern railway network was fleshed out. The first generation's proposals for improvement were aimed principally at opening up new avenues to capture unclaimed distant markets, as the citizens of Baltimore illustrated in 1827 when they predicted that if their B&O were built, "its benefits will be of the first importance, not to that mart alone, but to the general commerce of the country." For that reason, the city's citizens convinced themselves that their project was worthy of the "attention" of the "government of the union."[15]

Boosters strengthened their argument for the national good by pointing out that the East was already prosperous, certainly in contrast to the undeveloped West, and that the magic of railroads would transfer that affluence to the wilderness, which would in turn rebound to the benefit of easterners. Promoters therefore spent a great deal of time predicting what effects the East would have on the West, an exercise that, of course, also detailed the benefits the East would eventually enjoy. One suspects that promoters were realistic

I. W. Baldwin, *Manufacturer of Locomotive Steam Engines, Stationery Engines, Steamboat Engines, Railroad Machinery, Sugar Mills, &c. &c., Broad Street, Philadelphia.*

Little 4-2-0 engines such as this Baldwin product
were the mainstays of the railroads in the 1830s. The screening
at the top of the smokestack trapped some of the hot cinders.
(*American Railroad Journal*)

enough to carefully argue the mutual prosperity theme in order to attract western supporters to their various schemes. Eastern capitalists could expect little financial help from the westerners, but with the proper persuasion they could reap the benefits of political good will at all levels, and such tangible benefits as free rights of way, editorial support, state or territorial help, and cheaper supplies.

Tucked away in the folds of the era's literature were the writings of a few misanthropes who, although imbued with romantic notions of the West, drew somewhat different conclusions from their images and employed less appealing metaphors. One class noted for its jaundiced view of western prospects was the eastern financiers who hesitated to invest their capital in regions they had never heard of and had no interest in seeing. Westerners were always aware that they had to go east to beg for funds and then usually had to sell their securities there at large discounts that added to their roads' financial burdens. Poor quoted a writer for the Detroit *Free Press* who complained that "in the spring of 1846, we were in New York City, and heard an intelligent gentleman express surprise that capitalists could be found willing to invest money in a railroad away out west." Closer to home in an eastern West, the Gettysburg Rail Road meandered from that town all the way to someplace called Ripple's Tavern at the summit of South Mountain, Pennsylvania. When an 1837 legislative committee examined the road, it noted in its report that it had its "commencement in a wild, bleak, uninhabited, uninhabitable wilderness, and a termination in a diminutive village detached by at least forty-three miles from any public work." Later on the committee referred to the wilderness as "a frightful morass, impassable by man or beast, the basis of which is only known to Nature's God," definitely not an area ready to pour forth its bounty."[16]

Something of the same attitude permeated much of the literature on the Pacific railway before the Civil War. The monumental task of constructing such a railroad intimidated sponsors and opponents alike; the vast western reaches it had to cross were too forbidding. In the case of that dream, the West was merely a place to be gotten *across*, it was not the goal in itself. Transcontinental advocates thus often denigrated the lure of the wilderness, as did one such proponent in an 1853 issue of *Putnam's Monthly Maga-*

zine. The anonymous writer characterized a transcontinental as "rivalling in grandeur and surpassing in usefulness . . . the Pyramids of Egypt, the great Roman Military Roads, the Simplon of Napoleon." He was not overly imbued with romantic notions about the West, however; he spent more time discussing its problems: "the way is long, it is true," he admitted and "most of it through a wilderness," not to mention the innumerable streams and "the mountains among the highest" which would bedevil the road's construction gangs. The route would be costly and "the prospects of immediate gain from regions where there are no settlements, are not the most flattering," he said in one of the more gross understatements of the age. Although he admitted later that the Erie Canal was "dug for several hundred miles through an inhospitable wilderness" and attracted hordes of productive settlers, he thought, in the instance of the transcontinental, that "the time for the work has not yet arrived, and that we must await its coming; until the desolate territories through which it is to pass have been more thickly strewn with villages and cities," the inevitable signs of a commercial civilization. He looked out at the vast western vistas and saw only a great void.[17]

The doomsayers were a distinct minority. Most promoters, as Leo Marx has so ably pointed out, used the West as a metaphor to link the scientific and technological realities of the present with the rural, agrarian values of their Jeffersonian heritage. In doing so, writers superimposed discordant images without violating reason and common sense. They offered the American public its bright future and its comforting past at the same time; in fact, the one aided and abetted the other, promising continued growth and increased national prosperity. Moreover, the West's size and richness portended wealth for untold generations to come. In that sense, the image of the prolific West became a valued symbol of the nation's great potential.

CHAPTER 8

On Time

├─┼─┼─┼─┼─┼─┼─┼─┼─┼─┼─┼─┼─┼─┼─┤

I N the three decades before the Civil War, the American public enthusiastically embraced railroads, an invention that promised to expedite its pell-mell rush into the future. The new nation was in a hurry, in full pursuit of its Manifest Destiny. Never had a people pushed forward so fast. According to observers, they were in such a rush that they resented the time it took to eat; a perusal of the decadal censuses — and everyone seemed to read them — indicated that Americans even bred swiftly, and they always appeared to be heading off to discover what was over the horizon. Minor underscored the haste by labeling the period the "age of locomotion," while that keen observer of American ways, Domingo Faustino Sarmiento, declared that "if God were suddenly to call the world to judgment, He would surprise two-thirds of the population of the United States on the road like ants."[1]

The acceleration of events only exacerbated problems that already beset the young and cocksure but self-doubting republic. A healthy proportion of Sarmiento's Americans were on the move, flocking to states on the Gulf Coast and in the Northwest, as well as into such places as Arkansas and Iowa. The dispersal of population across two-thirds of the continent threatened to destroy what little political, economic, and cultural unity existed unless some bonds could be forged to draw the new regions into harmony with the older ones. Railway promoters assured Americans worried about these self-destructive tendencies that railroads would give them control of their destinies. The rails were the one instrument through which Americans could both hurry and solve the problems their own urgency created. It was a circular argument, of course, but with it, the rail advocates cleverly exploited that element in the national character that craved haste and change. They understood that time was of the essence for a people in a hurry, trying to solve the great national dilemmas while on the move. Railways, they argued, controlled time.

Railroad promoters concentrated on the topic to such an extent that ultimately they redefined the whole concept. They made time an essential part of American democracy — something moveable with a rising intrinsic value that everyone had. All benefited; Americans would be richer and, if they used it right, more free. After the railways' introduction nobody could ever look at the clock in quite the same way. Everything became amenable to chronological measurement, not just speed, but distance and capital, efficiency, profits, trustworthiness, safety, and reliability. In those pre-war years enthusiasts convinced the public that time was a commodity like salt or hogs that could be bought, sold, and saved. Paradoxically, however, these new notions about time introduced an added measure of discipline to a people that had traditionally worshipped at the altar of individualism. Across the land "railroad time" made everyone's life, no matter how isolated, a little more complex and a little more structured — like the railways themselves.

At the very simplest level, the utility of railroads was heavily contingent on their operating by some sort of schedule. People and produce had to be ready at the depot when the train was due to leave. Moreover, since railroads frequently operated trains in opposite directions on the same track, the only protection against disaster was a matter of timing; carefully "kept" time became at least a nominal guarantee that one train would not meet another around some blind curve. Before telegraphic dispatching — introduced in the early 1850s — scheduling was a major headache for all the larger roads. In 1846 Minor observed that Boston had ninety trains departing each day for one or another of twenty-five destinations, something like a ten-minute headway for a period of sixteen and a half hours, to say nothing of a presumably equal number of arrivals. While this density would not measure up to the less-than-ninety-second headway allowed rush-hour trains at New York's Grand Central Terminal in the early twentieth century, it was certainly formidable given the primitive operating practices of the day.[2]

Before the advent of airplanes and space travel, Americans grew up with a prominent image of the conductor swinging out from the vestibule, official pocket watch in hand, counting the seconds until time for the "highball." Terms like "on the clocker" or "on the tick" or the ubiquitous "on time" became clichés. By the 1850s everyone expected railroads to be on time, and management in turn expected employees to keep to "the advertised." Enduring legends grew about the exploits of engineers who, having been thrown "off schedule," performed heroic or foolhardy deeds to "make up time."

Even as the railroads were canonizing time, they were also creating time, or, more accurately, creating times. Formerly, if a long-distance traveler by stage, steamer, or canal boat arrived on the expected day, he was "on time." Each city, each town, each village, probably each individual as well, had a particular time. Frequently this time was designated "sun time," on the basis of the sun's passage across the local meridian. But as smaller railroads consolidated in the early 1850s and reached out for connections in the Midwest, officials found scheduling under such an anarchy of moment virtually impossible. Hence companies began designating "official time" by the local clock in some key city and setting depot clocks everywhere in something approaching synchronization. Every line thus created its own "railroad time," and travelers making connections entered a chronological maze understood only by the wizards who created it, a situation not alleviated until November 18, 1883, when all railroads adopted "standard time." Prior to that, railroads "set the time" for their respective environs, yet at a more fundamental level they also set the *tempo*. People congregated at the depot at "train time" not just to meet arrivals, see people off, and send or receive goods, but to catch up on local gossip or merely to "pass the time." The pulse of on-line communities beat in "perfect time" with that of the railroad, and the populace could not have escaped the standardization of time had it wanted to.[3]

Americans—farmers, most of them—had formerly responded to

time in essentially seasonal ways, in harmony with nature and the weather. Even eastern merchants fell under the same sway as they met at coffeehouses all up and down the coast in anticipation of favorable winds and tides to bring their vessels to port. Railroads broke nature's domination and compressed time. The arrival of the 1:40 every day or every other day was as regular as the tides, but under human command. As Americans began to understand the implications of that reality, they became fascinated with the idea of speed and of locomotives pulling trains at 4, 10, 15, 25, even 40 miles per hour, covering some point-to-point distance in "record time."

Speed remains, of course, an American preoccupation even to the present. Each weekend, somewhere in the country, people scrunch into strange-looking projectiles and speed down a precisely measured quarter-mile, the aim being to beat the "elapsed time" of their competitors. Devotees travel thousands of miles every year to spend, on a good day, less than two minutes watching three-year-old horses turn the circuit at Churchill Downs. The concept of speed has its own psychological manifestations as well. It took most of recorded history before a man finally ran a mile in less than four minutes; once the barrier was broken, however, almost anyone with a good pair of running shoes beat the mark. People now define both animate and mechanical capabilities in terms of seconds, minutes, and hours. They measure potentialities against an abstract definition of the possible, delineated in chronological terms. The origins of these notions go back a century and a half to an epoch when the railroads began to instill an awareness that time's limitations were not immutable.

There is, to be sure, ample evidence that Americans were already receptive to the idea of distance measured in time at the onset of the railroad era. In 1822, for example, the governor of Pennsylvania declared that turnpikes "promoted the convenience of the People" by "shortening distance." The people understood that his assertion, like DeWitt Clinton's statement that railroads "bring places and their inhabitants nigh together," was not to be taken literally; the point was that in a new technological world distance was more a matter of time than of measure. And by far the most promising technology was the railroad. In his 1830 *Treatise on Rail-Roads*, Thomas Earle elaborated various reasons why railroads were preferable to canals, several of which addressed elements of time and "celerity of transportation." Clearly a man in a hurry, Earle expressed impatience with canal and turnpike travel, bound to the "time honored" animal pace. He also had a notion that transport by means of speedier conveyances could save money for investors and travelers alike. Though Earle did not develop his argument in detail, his was a concept the public was just on the verge of accepting.[4]

When "sundry Citizens of Baltimore" met in 1827 to promote a railroad from their city to the Ohio River, their promises about time were quite specific: "The time saved by the railroad on each trip from the Ohio to Baltimore would be one hundred and fifty two hours, and . . . even at the rate of four miles an hour (which, it is believed, may be doubled) the whole distance may be performed in sixty two hours and a half."[5] Many enthusiasts who were then on hand undoubtedly lived to the Civil War period, when they could catch the train in Baltimore and ride to Wheeling in only nineteen hours at an average speed of twenty miles an hour even with forty-seven stops in between. A correspondent for *Niles' Weekly Register* had come close to forecasting such a reality when he predicted in 1829 that "the time will come, when a man may take breakfast with his family at Baltimore, and next day breakfast on the shores of the Ohio."[6]

Dreams of swift passage to far corners of the new nation were not the sole province of Baltimoreans. Niles published a letter in 1831 insisting that the child was already born "who could travel from Philadelphia to Boston in one day." Three years later a denizen of Philadelphia who had actually traveled to New York in just a few hours wrote the Philadelphia *Inquirer* that "this is undoubtedly one of the most startling facts connected with the progress and growth of Railroad traveling which has yet taken place in this section of the country." Someone signing himself "Jockey of York," who had been one of 141 passengers on a 1830 Christmas outing over the Charleston and Hamburg Railroad behind the *Best Friend of Charleston*, tried to give a taste of the experience to readers of the Charleston *Courier*: "we flew in the wings of the wind at the varied speed of fifteen to twenty-five miles an hour," he crowed, "annihilating 'time and space.'"[7]

While the Jockey indicated that he simply could not "take time" to reflect on the ramifications of "time and space," others both thought about the matter and wrote about it, thereby firing the popular fascination with railroads. It was an attraction not unlike that of 130 years later, when the nation committed a generous portion of its capital and talent to land a man on the moon. But railways, wrapped in that same glamor at their inception, possessed one important attribute the moon shots lacked—they were physically accessible to everyone. Something of the flavor of an enthusiast's perception can be seen in a piece that appeared in Niles's newspaper in 1831. With reference to the Liverpool and Manchester, the contributor (perhaps Niles himself) recounted that "these astonishing machines moved with almost the speed of the wind, going at the rate of from 15 to 25 miles an hour." Creating an analogous domestic setting, the account continued: "to see more clearly the curtailing influence of these [rail]roads on space and time, let us suppose that at less speed *by a third* than in *in this early stage* of locomotive experiment, has already been safely accomplished, a passenger was to set out on a rail road toward the west." This fictive traveler would "reach Lancaster in 2 hours, Pittsburg in 10 hours, New Orleans in less than 2 days, and return to Philadelphia within a week." For a Philadelphian in 1831 New Orleans might as well have been on the moon; one can scarcely overestimate the power of the notion that it could be reached in two days.[8]

The national ardor for redefining distance in terms of time quickened with completion of the early railroads. "*Science has conquered space*" Niles declared in 1835. "The people of places 1,000 miles apart, are nearer neighbors." *Scientific American* made a similar observation fourteen years later in noting that anyone who followed the progress of the railroad "must have been struck with its power of annihilating distance." By then, use of "annihilating" was commonplace in this context, as a word immediately evocative of the degree to which railways had—to quote Niles again—"change[d] the very nature of 'circumstances and time.'" "As we have said before," Niles continued, "distance will not be measured by *miles*, but by *hours* and *minutes*. 'It is ten hours to such a place, or 49 minutes to another.'"[9]

Measured in time, distance was not only shorter but—given "the right application of science"— *controllable.* After participating in opening ceremonies for the B&O's Washington branch, Niles fairly shouted the news that the distance from Baltimore was but "*two hours!*" and that the assembled crowd "rent the air with their acclamations *at this victory of science over time and space.*" Down in Savannah an editor was just as happy to explain, "the real distance between New-York and Philadelphia . . . is just the same as it was a hundred years ago,— but the relative distance is changed from seven days to seven hours."[10]

Their points were important; distance measured in the traditional way was real and immutable, but measured in hours and minutes, to quote Niles, it was rendered controllable. With the invention of the steam locomotive man was, for the first time in his history, able to dominate nature on a truly magnificent scale. It helped give haste a purpose in America: the locomotive was knitting the country together — fast — to enable Americans to transcend the limitations of time and distance that increasingly threatened the permanency of their union. The new conceptions of time and space nourished the idea of perpetual progress that later grew to manifold proportions under the guise of Manifest Destiny. In fact, such redefinitions made Manifest Destiny possible, adding an important element to the American character.

The redefinition of time also augmented one of the national character's older aspects. Benjamin Franklin's aphorism that "time is money," for example, took on additional meaning in the railroad era. As early as his third issue Minor quoted the old sage, linking him to the approaching railway revolution. Niles, too, summoned up Franklin in explaining why "passengers will not travel on canals, when they can pass over railroads, if they have business to attend to, or time has value to them." Correctly assuming that nobody would admit that his time had no value, railroad promoters hammered home the idea that everyone would profit from the great time-saving machine on rails.[11]

Dr. Caldwell had given that whole question a great deal of thought and arrived at an equation which read time = money = profits for all. Projecting the experience of the Liverpool and Manchester on an American situation, Caldwell pictured the intimate relationship that would develop between the cities of Lexington and

NORRIS' LOCOMOTIVE WORKS.

BUSHHILL, SCHUYLKILL SIXTH-ST., PHILADELPHIA.

THE UNDERSIGNED Manufacture to order Locomotive Steam Engines of any plan or size.
Their shops being enlarged, and their arrangements considerably extended to facilitate the speedy execution of work in this branch, they can offer to Railway Companies unusual advantages for prompt delivery of Machinery of superior workmanship and finish.

Connected with the Locomotive business, they are also prepared to furnish, at short notice, Chilled Wheels for Cars of superior quality.

Wrought Iron Tyres made of any required size—the exact diameter of the Wheel Centre, being given, the Tires are made to fit on same without the necessity of turning out inside.

Iron and Brass castings, Axles, etc., fitted up complete with Trucks or otherwise.

NORRIS, BROTHERS

By the turn of the century Norris built heavier engines
with smaller driving wheels for freight work
and lighter locomotives with high wheels to speed passengers
who needed to save time to their destinations.
(*American Railroad Journal*, Mar. 15, 1851)

Louisville when a railroad connection was finished. Were a beau in Louisville to fall in love with a beauty in Lexington, he would not have "to beseech to gods" to

> . . . annihilate both time and space,
> And Make two lovers happy. . . .

Having seen to streamlining the process of "making time," the good doctor became at once serious, declaring that in "the transaction of business, in distant places, much time, as well as money, will be saved by Railroads. And the portion of each article, thus gained, may be applied to very important purposes."[12]

Caldwell's ideas about purpose centered on "cultivation of the mind," though most railroad proponents had less lofty aims. "A New-York Citizen" who wrote Minor in 1835 noted that America was a country where "delay is brooked with impatience, and increased speed paid for liberally by the impatient traveler." Time could command a premium, increasing the profits of those who controlled the time machine. Minor himself (much to his consternation) thought that Boston was far ahead of New York or any other city in adopting "these *time* and *money-saving machines.*" A staunch advocate of extending the Harlem Railroad to Albany in order to stop Boston from stealing New York's trade, he attempted to sell this project to all classes by asserting that railroads "contribute largely to the business facilities of the people and particularly the *poor*, with whom time is *capital.*"[13]

The idea that the unskilled had nothing to sell but their time was long a prime motivating force in the formation of labor unions, but in antebellum times it was a novel concept that the poor would benefit from faster transportation because it would enable them to save time, their "capital." As railroads spread across the Alleghenies, the potential for "saving" both time and money expanded. The directors of the Steubenville and Indiana, in their first annual report in 1850, promised that most travel between Pittsburgh and Cincinnati would be diverted from the Ohio River because the trip would be a day shorter. They were certain that people would be willing to spend money to save time that would enable them to make money.[14]

Railway promoters did a masterful job of integrating the new form of travel with prominent aspects of the American character.

They proclaimed that Americans were a people on the march toward progress and that the journey was being made at "double-time." Faster was better. Speed shortened distances, improved communications, put money in everyone's pockets, pulled the country together, and accelerated its movement toward unity. Railroads controlled the key ingredient — time — essential to realize each of those vital goals.

Time, however, had its oppressive aspects as well. Americans had to learn to live within ever more rigid temporal constraints, especially those who labored in the land's mills and factories. Factory time was created alongside railroad time, and workers were disciplined to react to bells and whistles. Railroads not only standardized and speeded up time, they "annihilated" hours that traditionally had been dedicated to leisure. No American, no matter how remote his locale, was immune to these changes. Even if he were outside the market economy, his habits of mind, the way he looked at his world, his very character, changed radically. His horizons were both expanded and narrowed by the redefinition of time; by the time promoters finished with the subject, nothing was ever again quite the same.[15]

CHAPTER 9

"At What Cost?"

OILS
FOR RAILROADS,
MACHINERY AND BURNING.

MANUFACTURERS OF
OILS AND CANDLES,
154 Front St., corner of Maiden Lane, New York,
Devote *special attention* to the preparation of the
best Oil for Burning, Machinery, and for
LUBRICATING ENGINES AND CARS,
at the *lowest prices.* Orders promptly filled.
June 1, 1863.

Despite promoters' brilliant successes in pitching their appeals to the most vulnerable areas of the American character, there were always those who adamantly resisted them. Publicists could focus attention on the larger picture and show that railways symbolized the American dream; they could even argue all they wanted that rails were vital to the nation's preservation; but still some people remained unmoved by their entreaties. These skeptics preferred to exploit the gaps between advocates' promises and the locomotive's reality. For them all images and metaphors were woefully inadequate to explain the differences between expectations and reality. The objectors loved to publicize instances where the innovation did not do everything its backers promised or when it brought unpleasant side-effects. Generally they gave short shrift to the promoters' long-range promises and concentrated instead upon more immediate consequences of building railways. They were no more short-sighted than their contemporaries; they just had strong personal grievances against a specific railroad or else saw railways as threats to their personal well-being.

Many such nonbelievers responded with an almost macabre glee to the gory accidents that plagued the new invention. Readers especially seemed to relish those caused by willful ignorance on the part of railroad employees, such as one explosion described in *Niles' Register* in 1831, in which "the engineer was severely scalded, one negro badly wounded and two slightly." The piece continued to explain that one of the wounded men "was the fireman, *who caused the accident*, by pressing on the *safety valve* to prevent the escape of steam." And all over the country drunks exhibited a proclivity to sleep off their binges on railroad tracks. Given the nation's prodigious alcohol consumption and the fact that this illicit sleeping was generally done at night when locomotive illumination was at best very primitive, railway accident rates rose accordingly. The Athens (Ga.) *Southern Banner* reported in 1845, almost happily, that one such miscreant "was horribly mangled" by a passing train. Livestock had the same urge to spend time standing between the newly laid tracks. In 1847 a New Jersey farmer, one William Cubberly, saw his bull prematurely slaughtered by a Camden and Amboy train. Cubberly was so incensed that he placed an obstruction on the track to derail the next train. He was caught and fined one hundred dollars. In one of the stranger accidents, an engineer on the Columbia Railroad west of Philadelphia in 1835 was taken aback to see a bull "coming at the top of his speed, his tail stuck right into the air, his head down, as if for immediate attack." Stunned, the engineer stopped the train and the bull smashed into the engine. When the animal retreated for another attack, the engineer started the train and the bull struck somewhere behind the engine; the last the passengers saw of the animal, he was rolling into the ditch. The people who gloated over such stories formed an early coterie of anti-railroad folk whose images of the new industry were at variance with those so ably put forward by that era's promoters.[1]

Wagoners, canalers, innkeepers, and livery stable owners near the lines of the proposed routes, who found the new invention threatened their livelihoods, more fiercely resisted the editorial blandishments of early railway enthusiasts. As early as 1824, internal improvement commissioners in Pennsylvania realized that there would be opposition to a projected line of canals and railways across the state. They reacted with numerous statistics showing that the cost of shipping by canal would be much lower than by turnpike and pointed out that this "will take the wagoning off our turnpikes";

but they noted that "if it does, the country will be great gainers by the advanced prices they will get at the canal market." The commissioners also had some sage, if unwelcome, advice for those who made their living from the turnpikes, advising that "the wagoners must change their occupations, and the horses be put to farm work."[2]

Wagoners who lost their jobs to canals and railways remained an embittered lot, releasing their pent-up hatreds in songs that collectively became known as "Wagoners' Songs." Most are untitled and their tunes have been lost, but their verses clearly indicate that their writers marched to a different metaphorical drummer. One middle Atlantic composition of this genre starts:

> Oh, Its once I made money by driving my team,
> But now all is hauled on the railroad by steam.
> May the devil catch the man that invented the plan,
> For its ruined us poor wagoners, and every other man.

Another, attributed to the Rev. John Pierpont Morgan, grandfather of J.P. Morgan, showed more imagination:

> We hear no more the clanking hoof,
>   And stage-coach rattling by;
> For the steam-king rules the travelled world,
>   And the pike is left to die.
> The grass creeps over the flinty path,
>   And the stealthy daisies steal
> Where once the stage-horse' day by day,
>   Lifted his iron heel.

And he continued for another four verses in the same vein.[3]

A distinctly more bitter ballad, called the "Conestoga Wagoners" was sung to the tune of "Green on the Cape." Its chorus set the tone:

> Come, — all ye bold wagners turn out man by man,
> That's opposed to the railroad or any such a plan,
> 'Tis once I made money by driving my team,
> But the goods are now hauled on the rail-road by steam.

Unlike many, this ballad suggested specific grievances against the railways. For example, it pointed out that track "spoils our plantations where it may cross," and the writer was sophisticated enough to notice the railways' secondary effects when he put to music the notion that the railroad "ruins our markets, so we can't sell a hoss." The ballad also demonstrated a clear class-consciousness, especially where it predicted the railroad "ruins wheelwrights, blacksmiths, and every other trade," concluding that "it fills our country full of just a lot of great rich men." The ballad suggested the wagoners were not very enthralled with the Jeffersonian yeoman-farmer image either:

> Come, all ye bold wagoners, that have got good wives,
> Go home to your farms and there spend your lives.
> When your corn is all cribbed and your small grain
> is sowed,
> You'll have nothing else to do but just to curse the
> damned railroad.[4]

In Pennsylvania at least, the wagoners did more than just sing a lament for their obsolescence; they put political pressure on the state legislature and governor so that in 1837 the governor asked the lawmakers for an appropriation to help the wagoners. The chief executive cleverly asked for aid to turnpikes, arguing that the state's "wagoners as a distinct race are rapidly disappearing from many parts of the State, yet, they are still the main reliance of several counties, either inaccessible to, or yet unreached by canals and rail roads." The governor thereby placated representatives from remote districts taxed to support state works and an enfranchised occupational group threatened with extinction.[5]

Pennsylvania commissioners in 1824 had predicted the demise of many innkeepers, but held out the hope that while " a few innkeepers may suffer a partial loss, . . . it will be very partial if they keep good taverns, for the facilities given to commerce by the canal, will increase intercourse prodigiously." They reasoned that improved transportation encouraged an increase in business along older parallel routes such as the turnpikes and that, with the heavy wagons gone, the roads would be smoother, thus luring more folk to travel them and put up at the inns.[6]

There is a dearth of similar literature for this period written by canal advocates against railroads. The canal mania, however, coincided with the beginnings of the railway movement, and for the decade of the 1830s promoters of both canals and railroads built apace. Canal mileage in that decade on which Andrew Jackson left his indelible political imprint almost tripled from 1,277 to 3,326. Railroads may have been the rage in many parts of the nation, but when the census-takers counted mileage for the 1840 decadal tabulation, they found the United States had only *two* more miles of railway than canal. In was in the 1840s that the "steam-king" took his throne. In that decade, only a little more than 300 miles of canal were dug, while over 5,500 miles of rails were spiked down. Moreover, where railways paralleled canals, as in Pennsylvania, New York, and Ohio, they did not always drive the ditches from business and threaten canalers' jobs. The Erie Canal's tonnage, for example, peaked *after* the Civil War. Pennsylvania, Ohio, and Indiana canal systems did not survive, but many continued in business long after mid-century, hauling heavy, low-tariff tonnage, leaving the railways the passenger business and the lighter, more lucrative freight on which time was a premium.[7]

Canal opposition to railways tended to divide into those who focused on details of finance, policy, or management of the rails, and the more harmless rantings of those who were drawn to the canals for emotional, philosophical, or romantic reasons. A fine example of the latter appeared in an oft-reprinted anonymous article entitled "A Canal Stockholder's Outburst" that first saw the light of day in an 1830 edition of the Vincennes, Indiana, *Western Sun.* The author was certain that twenty miles per hour on railways would "set the whole world a-gadding." Nobody would stay put and work steadily; instead, the canaler claimed that with railroads "all local attachments will be at an end." The writer also proposed that rails would "upset all the gravity of the nation" and encourage those with personal vendettas to "steal off to the Rocky Mountains" to fight their illegal duels. Obviously a creditor himself, he predicted that "a set of bailiffs mounted on Bombshells would not overtake an absconded debtor." Therefore, he opined "I go for beasts of burden; it is more primitive and scriptural, and suits a moral and religious people better. None of your hop-skip-and-jump whimsies for me!"[8]

Much opposition to railroads arose from people fearful that railways would somehow upset their tight, secure little worlds. The Internal Improvements Committee of the Pennsylvania legislature in

Rail shipments of bulk products such as cotton
threatened the livelihoods of wagoners and canalers.
(Brown, *The History of the First Locomotives in America*)

1830, when discussing the Main Line, referred to this conservative element when it warned that any "scheme of improvement may be burthened, delayed, and perhaps frustrated, by selfish, local attachments of collateral connexions." Four years later it broadened its indictment of parochial interests when it complained that the state works were hindered by "the vigilant, jealous, and suspicious eyes of those who, from motives arising from local, political or personal causes, are interested in thwarting their execution or hindering their success."[9]

Some of these opponents were simply congenital skeptics, but many were sophisticated, urbane folk who had to be persuaded that railroads were worthy of their attention. The author of an extended review of Poussin's *Chemins de Fer Americains* in an 1837 issue of the *North American Review* was incredulous that, at that late date, many articulate, rich, Bostonians regarded those who advocated a railway from Boston to Albany "not merely with distrust, but literally as persons of unsound mind." He was dismayed that a "great mass of sober men — those who mutually look to one another for lessons of prudence, who fully understand the mystery of making profitable investments, and who lead the counsels of legislative bodies" remained unconvinced that railways could benefit their city. With a tone of resignation he reserved for the most obdurate, he concluded that "they boldly shut their minds against conviction, with the intrepidity of men who believe that an appeal to their understandings is but a prelude to an attack upon their pockets."[10]

On the other end of the spectrum were those people convinced that railways caused the 1837 panic and the ensuing depression, the worst the nation had witnessed, who felt the railway companies already had attacked "their pockets." They took their convictions into the state political arenas, demanding investigations, and made such headway that Minor wrote an editorial attacking the trend. He did not argue railroads were innocent, rather he took the stance that "the want of correct statistics of railroads in the United States, and the outrageous assertions recently made in our legislative halls, as to their unprofitableness, have had the effect of prejudicing the minds of a large portion of the community against this most valuable species of improvement." It was the exact argument reformers would make fifty years later when they assured the public that railroad reform would come about as soon as people knew the true facts and established state railway commissions to collect and publish them. Even the language used against railroads in the 1830s was reminiscent of that employed later in the century, as Minor reported that "speculations," "losing concerns," "Public evils," and similar catchwords had been repeated and dwelt upon.[11]

While Minor thought that the frustration of hard times called forth the harsh public outcry, some of it was prompted by a wide-spread distrust of all corporations. Many across the country called for publicly owned improvements to serve the general good, especially in transportation and municipal services. There was little room for compromise; opinions on both sides were strongly held and the literature was often emotional. Even usually bland legislative committees showed an unaccustomed flair when addressing the controversial topic of public versus private ownership. Witness an 1835 Pennsylvania Senate report on the Lehigh navigation and coal trade which asserted that private "companies, like individuals, will endeavor always to pursue their own interests; and if they believe they can realize a greater profit by engaging themselves in a particular branch of trade, . . . they will of course embark in the trade, and endeavor to monopolize it."[12]

Nothing could arouse the wrath of anti-corporate forces faster than the suggestion that an out-of-state corporation be allowed to do business on their native turf; that brought forth the combined ire of those wedded to the protection of local interests and those who hated all private companies. One of the era's most colorful debates took place in the mid-1840s, when the B&O applied for a charter to build a line to Pittsburgh, with that town's blessing, to tap its trade for Baltimore. Fifteen years earlier, when the Baltimore and Susquehanna Rail Road Company, a Maryland creation, applied to the Quaker Commonwealth for the right to enter its domain, a house committee responded that "the expediency of placing the leading roads of a state in the hands of corporations, has in all ages been questioned; and some of the wisest statesmen inculcate the maxim, that roads and canals are to be made by the state, and kept in the hands of the state." Having so defined the debate, the lawmakers had no trouble deciding the merits of the case, pointing out that it was "believed that the incorporation of persons

This 1839 poster, circulated in Philadelphia, combined anti-monopoly feelings with a fear of out-of-state corporations. (Historical Pictures Service, Chicago)

who are not citizens of Pennsylvania, . . . with power to raise a revenue from the people, and who may contrive to conduct their business beyond the vigilance and reach of our laws, ought not to engage the serious attention of the legislature."[13]

One of the most thoroughgoing attacks on private corporations in the literature was launched from Texas, where Lorenzo Sherwood penned a devastating diatribe against private ownership of transportation, published in an 1855 issue of *DeBow's Review*. Sherwood's timing was interesting, as Texas's internal improvements then stood about where the eastern seaboard states had been two decades earlier. The Lone Star state boasted not a single mile of railroad in 1850, but soon began to build railways northward from Galveston and Houston, opening the first 32 miles in 1854 and registering a full 306 operating miles for the marshals to count in the next census. When Sherwood wrote, however, his state had less than 50 miles of railway open.[14]

The Texan was livid because northeastern states were selling their public works to private corporations. By the mid-fifties Indiana, Illinois, and Michigan had fled the improvements business and, because they had done so, Sherwood thought, "the dominion of corporate monopoly is established in all of them." He believed it was more than simply happenstance that the corporate world was in the ascendancy; it was a conspiracy of sorts. "From 1842, onward," the Texan asserted, "corporators have been sedulously and industriously at work, to get rid of the effect of State competition." They did so, he claimed, because "they find themselves . . . with all their slanders and machinations, unable to stand against its effects." Despite the fact that public works carried more tonnage at less cost everywhere, he was sure that these truths could not be effectively spread before the public because "corporators, always mercenary in prosperity and desperate in adversity, desire the interested advocacy of the press, [and] they have the power to make it so." Not only that, but Sherwood was sure "if they require interested legislators, cabinets, or governors, they have the power to make them so." With that point he really warmed to his subject:

Almost everything shows degeneracy before railway financiering. Premiers, lords, and commons, are no more suffered to escape contamination than the needy politician. Few men have ever fully contemplated the political Jesuitism of this vast power; and fewer still have ventured on the attempt to grapple with its influence. There is but one arena, and one tribunal on earth where it is possible to check its overgrowth, and awe it into subjection, or even decency. *That tribunal is the people.*

Sherwood regularly read the *American Railroad Journal* out on the Texas frontier; he kept up with national railroad news and even published a letter in the paper. Based on his evaluation of national trends, he concluded the only way to avoid corporate excesses was for Texas to build a public works system and change its state constitution to make shareholders in private corporations liable for their company's debts. Then, he claimed with a Texas flavor, "we would have no more trouble from them than we would from mosquitoes and horseflies, when the mercury stood at zero."[15]

In a visceral sense, Sherwood, from his remote western observation post, understood the national debate that raged between those who feared corporate excesses and those who welcomed a freer, more competitive brand of capitalism. While both sides could at times pay obeisance to the national unity image the debate itself seriously undermined it. Many observers predicted that private ownership was the wave of the future, and railway enthusiasts were hard at work raising the means to conduct the public's transportation for private ends. Railroads and private enterprise were becoming one and the same in the public's mind, but as Louis Hartz has noted in his *Economic Policy and Democratic Thought: Pennsylvania 1776–1860,* the battles between state and corporate forces would be sharp and furious. In all the clamor the metaphors that had melded public and private interests would be radically transformed.[16]

Beneath the debates was an underlying uneasiness about the wisdom of trusting private or even joint stock corporations to operate in the public's interest. In his annual message in January 1840, Governor David R. Porter of Pennsylvania devoted a long passage to this problem. He left no doubt where he stood on the issue, explaining that "a few persons collectively had been specially delegated, by Acts of Assembly, with powers and immunities denied to the rest of the community, and thus have numerous monopolies been created, not only to reveal but to trample down all individual efforts and enterprise." Having thus defined a corporation, the rest was easy. Porter claimed one company almost biblically begat another until there were so many that the legislature should take stock of what was happening. He admitted there was not much he could do about corporations already in existence "unless their own misconduct requires it," an idea echoed in Teddy Roosevelt's so-called New Nationalism some seventy-two years later. The whole system, Porter thought, had to be reformed. On the local level the editor of the Worcester (Massachusetts) *Palladium* expressed the same sentiments three years later when he complained about the intent shown by the signs in the town that read "Look out for engine while the Bell Rings." The editor claimed the liability for grade-crossing accidents should be the other way around, explaining "and then the *corporations* must look out for the *people* — and not the *people* for the *corporations*."[17]

A considerable number of people agreed with the *Palladium*'s editor and remained immune to the railway fraternity's blandishments. These nay-sayers kept looking at the smaller picture and asking "at what price?" While they were unable to slow the national infatuation for railways in those first two decades, they eventually had their day. The objections they kept alive through that first burst of railway enthusiasm became more popular in the 1850s and undermined the industry's national unity metaphor. Many Americans became aware in that decade that corporate officers were motivated as much by greed as by any altruistic desire to better the lot of all citizens.

Death of the National Unity Image

├─┼─┼─┼─┼─┼─┼─┼─┼─┼─┼─┼─┼─┼─┼─┤

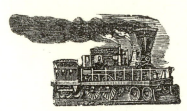

T HE railroad world changed in the 1850s, and so did its self-image. As the industry grew and matured it faced a host of new problems and opportunities. The most noticeable change was the fierce competition among roads, especially in the East where the rail network was almost finished. The competition forced managers to struggle to keep their profit-and-loss statements healthy. They had to devise new strategies for survival, including expansion, mergers, higher tolls, streamlined organizations, more disciplined labor, and increased attention to receipts and expenditures. Their attention was also drawn into politics as they sought charter reforms, helpful state legislation, tax relief, and, in some states, permission to charge rates based on their actual costs of carriage. These concerns narrowed the railway leaders' focus; their loyalties and jobs depended on how well they guided their companies through the dangers that were everywhere. The managers' reactions fragmented the industry and set company against company, locality against locality, and region against region in a process that paralleled and fed into events in the nation's political arena. When rail leaders' policies were designed only to enhance their own corporate fortunes, they guaranteed the industry's divorce from any overall image that embodied the country's hopes for unity and happiness.

The language used in railroad offices mirrored industry changes. By the early 1850s promoters had already dropped the harmonious and friendly metaphors and began to sprinkle their writings with a rancor that showed they were less interested in what their railways could do for the Union than in how they could serve their own best interests. Part of this change was due to the fact that, as railroads matured, the men who managed them became more important than the men who had advocated their construction. The men who spoke for the industry in that sixth decade were looking at the business from the inside and were more concerned with its daily workings. They lacked the larger view and flair that had served promoters for decades, and those who still read rail literature noted that the industry had become more self-serving. Even those outside the business changed. Poor wrote a piece in 1852 in which he formally laid the national unity image to rest. Railroads, he asserted, were "merely *commercial* enterprises, and are to be conducted upon commercial principles, which never sanction an enormous sacrifice for a contingent good."[1]

Some of those "commercial enterprises" had grown to a scale that Americans could not have earlier imagined. Promoters routinely issued calls for tens of millions of dollars for construction, hundreds of thousands of acres of public lands, thousands of laborers, and millions of tons of iron. Stephen Girard, the country's first recognized millionaire, was only a dozen years dead before businessmen were spending ten times that amount of money yearly. That capital, however, built 17,317 finished miles of road by the start of the decade and had another 12,526 under construction. Railroads already operating grew almost as fast. The Pennsylvania Railroad was then worth over three million dollars and employed in excess of three thousand men, more than the state it served. The company even had a full time lobbyist to handle political chores when the legislature was in session. And a lot more companies entered the competitive fray. Where there had only been 172 chartered roads in 1850, ten years later the number had swelled to 464. The high fixed costs, the great number of workers dependent upon the companies for their support, and the heated competition narrowed managers' vision. They had to maintain regular dividends and high levels of service to keep their directors and stockholders happy and to survive. That was more important than all the promotional rhetoric in the world about serving national needs. Rail executives did not simply become more narrow-minded and selfish; their primary tasks required them to concentrate their interests on practical problems and on the welfare of the companies for which they were responsible.[2]

The general public in the East became less enchanted with railroads during that decade. As the business separated from national desires for a greater measure of unity and stopped using the language that eased popular fears about weaknesses in the American character, a gulf widened between the general public and the industry. There was a gradual loss of the sense that Americans were metaphorically a "railroad people," and in its place appeared a measure of distrust. That estrangement grew as the industry's literature became more self-serving and frequently too technical. The public lost interest in it or could no longer understand it. When Poor admitted to his readers as early as 1852 that "railroading is now reduced to a science," he meant that it was becoming more technical. He was not referring to the former metaphorical notion that science was progress and any literate man could understand it. By midcentury magicians of the industrial age spoke a different language from ordinary mortals. Technical works such as Herman Haupt's classic, *General Theory of Bridge Construction*, or his article entitled "On the Resistance of the Vertical Plates of Tubular Bridges" were not an easy evening's read for anyone and totally incomprehensible for most. As discussions of railroad affairs became more unintelligible to the average reader, they came to seem conspiratorial and even frightening. Poor understood something of this problem, especially as it affected those trying to raise construction funds. His unfailing advice to promoters attempting to allay such fears was always to be candid with the public and to open company books for general inspection. He was less successful, however, in bridging the gap between the interested public and the new profession of men who interpreted what he thought was "emphatically the age of machinery," although Poor, himself, understood what they were trying to say.[3]

Some rail officials alienated their readers by saying too little. In their early years they tried to keep the public informed about their companies' policies through annual reports. They were often veritable mother lodes of information on corporate thinking, financial problems, and hopes, written for the average citizen and frequently published verbatim in local newspapers. The reports were one of the chief avenues of accountability from the managers and their directors and shareholders to local politicians and the general public. As lines of accountability changed and competition intensified, however, such candid annual reports became dangerous. By the Civil War, managers mastered the art of writing excessively long statistical compendiums that said more but told the public less. The annual renderings became almost a literary genre, self-congratulatory, and rarely given to metaphorical flights of fancy that might catch the readers' interest. Rather than imparting a sense that railways were engaged in a great national task, the reports recited corporate triumphs and set blame for policies that had gone awry.

As the rail industry grew in size and became more distant from the public's everyday concerns, it lost that sense of being the underdog that had long endeared it to the American public. Americans could readily identify with the idea of a courageous David fighting vast odds, and such an image enabled them to champion the tiny locomotives struggling against nature's worst elements. Those bonds between railroads and the public were everywhere daily strengthened in the early years by personal contact along the railway; train crews stopped frequently to take on wood and water, ate in local hotels, chatted with residents, brought news and gossip from afar to trade over a mug of the locality's pride, and were in turn respected for their courage and talents. With the development of more powerful and sophisticated locomotives, however, Americans increasingly saw railway workers only from trackside when the express flew by, a much less intimate relationship. An unidentified writer was thinking about this phenomenon in 1853 when he described a 444 mile trip from New York City to Buffalo that he made in only 14.5 hours. "At this rate of speed," he advised, "the landscape, and various villages and cities on the route, dashed past us with such velocity and appeared and disappeared in such rapid succession that we could scarcely get a distinct idea of one scene before it was displaced by another." Even allowing for the usual hyperbole inherent in such accounts, Americans were becoming a blur as they sped past one another.[4]

This horizontal boilered steam engine was
a typical midcentury product. A few railroads at that late date
still offered their engine crews no protection from the elements.
Cabs were universal by the end of that decade, however.
(*American Railroad Journal*, Oct. 8, 1853)

Railroad companies were becoming something of a legal blur as well, a fact that frightened a Pennsylvania Senate Committee in 1845. The committee explained that a "large majority of the citizens of Pennsylvania look with a jealous eye upon all mammoth corporations. They believe that special privileges, and special immunities, should not be conferred upon any portion of the people at the expense of the rest." Earlier the committee referred to an out-of-state corporation as " irresponsible and soulless," a characterization that many throughout the nation would not have hesitated to apply to any large company. In the absence of federal incorporation laws, many Americans were edgy about losing legal control of companies as they "escaped" into neighboring states that exercised no jurisdiction over "foreign" companies. Ralph Waldo Emerson wrestled with this problem in 1856 after he noticed that the Michigan Southern ran "through four sovereign states"; that made it, he thought, a "judicial being, which has no judicial sovereign."[5]

Emerson was ahead of his time, however; most Americans in the 1850s disagreed with him. They believed that railroads were creatures of their important cities and that the urban areas were using the rails as weapons in their battles for more trade. This was the period of intense urban competition that contributed to the national unity image's demise. All up and down the Atlantic Coast people discovered that their cities were not benefitting equally from the railway revolution; it was clear by the mid-century census that New York City had far outdistanced other eastern also-rans. Seaboard hatreds intensified as city fathers used railroads to threaten their neighbors.

These rivalries caused much change within the industry. The New York Central, consolidated into one corporate entity in 1853, was the product of New York fears that its prominence was threatened. Philadelphians meanwhile became convinced that only if they pushed their rails to Erie and into the Midwest could they outflank the colossus to the north. Bostonians, a step behind in the race, staked their hopes and their state treasure on the Hoosac Tunnel route to shorten the run from Albany, where Boston interests could siphon more trade away from the historic Hudson River channel. Older coastal cities fired statistical salvos at each other, and their literature reflected the increased bitterness of the heightened competition.

Railway promoters no longer suggested helping a rival's improvement because its completion would redound to everyone's benefit. Instead, in a trend that paralleled internal railroad developments, city fathers measured any transportation scheme by the yardstick of what that route would do for their city. They too lowered their sights and narrowed their focus. Eastern promoters, however, were still willing to help midwestern cities, rapidly becoming regional commercial hubs, in order to tie them to eastern markets by an "iron girdle," as one St. Louis devotee of metaphors described it.[6] The rhetoric of conflict that spilled out into the Midwest overlaid the national unity image still popular there. The intra- and inter-regional urban struggles were everywhere mean; and they also rendered policy making inordinately complicated for railway presidents on the larger roads. Luckily, however, the period of intense urban rivalries was short. It began only after the national unity image was in tatters and ended soon after the war, when railroad managers brought the cities under their sway.

Railways did more than simply mirror the growing divisiveness in the character of America; they helped prompt it. As the rails reached out for increased trade, they drew states and regions together, rather than the nation. As they bound their locales with iron economic ties, political cooperation, sometimes forced by powerful railway managers, soon followed. Regional centralization, loyalty, and pride were natural offshoots of this stage of rail expansion. Those promoters who had long advertised the national benefits that would follow rail construction overlooked the fact that in the initial phase they would be local and regional instead. The rails' major effect, however, was out beyond the Ohio and Mississippi rivers, where the east-west rail net severed western reliance on the river trade and bound its business tightly to free northern cities.

Like the railway officials, regional politicians, capitalists, and boosters everywhere became more self-serving. For a short time they viewed the great railroads as avenues expressly designed to serve major cities rather than more vague national goals. Railroad executives adopted the language of that image to an extent when they referred to the "Boston roads," or "New York route," or "Philadelphia lines." They also adopted the acrimonious language of their competitive world and acted in concert with it. The increasingly virulent corporate and urban competition spewed its malevolent poison over the countryside where it spilled into the national arena, just as surely as the rancor of the slave debates seeped into boardrooms and city councils. The new railroad leaders, less accountable to their companies' owners and to the public, acted in accord with the images that prompted their language, and declared war upon one another. The national unity image was dead.

Birth of the Corporate State Image

THE railway world was a microcosm for many of the ills that beset the national character in that decade prior to the Civil War. While sectional political leaders battled in America's highest councils for control of national policies, so too did regional railroad executives fight to control the economic welfare of large numbers of people. The moods in corporate headquarters turned as angry and disputatious as those in Congress. The industry divided into friendly and unfriendly competing camps that discarded national goals for more selfish policies. The language railway leaders adopted revealed they had replaced the old national unity concept with a new image, that of the corporate state, that was more in accord with their companies' situations and the world outside them.

Many railroad officials, especially presidents, had drawn corporate power into their hands until they had become in every respect rulers over their businesses. As their industry became more complex, technical decisions were increasingly left to them, while boards of directors and stockholders' committees gladly relinquished oversight of companies' affairs. The ambitious railway executives who filled those power vacuums began to view themselves as sovereigns wielding vast authority over their business domains while beset on all sides by the same dangers that assailed their political counterparts. Many managers, especially on the larger roads, acted as if they were political leaders of small states. They determined who they would serve and, more importantly, who they would not; they devised policies that affected thousands of people, set rates that were a tax on the transport of goods, often deliberated in secret, speculated in their own companies' securities, and sought to cooperate with each other while escalating levels of corporate conflict. The railroad's new image, which would one day prompt Mark Twain to refer to railway magnates as "barons," was not yet fully outlined in the 1850s, though its metaphors were already becoming popular.

The image's most notable manifestation in the early literature was the roads' officers increasing identification with corporate rather than national goals. Symbolically, the president of the United States, Millard Fillmore, announced that shift. By the time Fillmore attended the Erie Railroad's grand-opening festivities in 1851, he had quite unconsciously absorbed the metaphorical changes sweeping across his land. As the *Weekly Baltimore Patriot* reported, the honored speaker at the mandatory banquet hoisted his glass and praised, "The New York & Erie Railroad—the great private enterprise of the age." The New Yorker had traveled across the state not to honor a national project, but to salute a large corporation. It was an important distinction. The president recognized that the railroad had a primary obligation to pursue its private ends. The chief executive probably assumed, however, that the company's best interests and the public's needs would coincide for the greater national good, taking comfort in the last remaining link between the old and the new images.[1]

In this process of transforming the venerable image, railway executives gained the power to define what constituted the common good. By the 1850s railroad managers all over the East began to characterize it as that which contributed to their roads' welfare. Because railways served their sponsoring commercial interests, who set the economic and cultural tones for their respective communities, rail officers narrowed their concepts of public and good. In so doing they set the metaphorical pyramid upside down. Interestingly, Minor had stumbled upon this redefinition back in 1845 when he wrote an editorial curiously entitled "Advancing Backwards." In it, he posited a truism that was intimately related to the reigning metaphor of earlier years, namely that "the time *will* come when legislators, both municipal and State, will learn that the lesser must yield to the greater good." Without pause, Minor continued to define the "greater good" as that of "the business of a commercial city, and of a whole community, [which] must be subject to the fewest possible *restraints*."[2]

The roots of this notion were sunk deep in the literature and reached back to at least a decade earlier, when all over the country railway advocates began to tout the advantages of private railroads over public ownership of improvements. In North Carolina the 1843 legislature debated that vital question, and the lawmakers finally agreed with the allegations that railroads' "construction has occasioned a heavy loss to the State, without an adequate return; and that, consequently, they deserve not the fostering care of the public."[3]

Less than two years later, Minor took a hard look at the host of bankruptcies bedeviling the railroad industry. Against the backdrop of a national depression he concluded that "hereafter, there is every reason to believe, that the public works of this country will be conducted on correct principles," a portent that the editor was going to narrow his newspaper's emphasis from serving national ends to outlining proper management techniques needed to make business pay. "And we think we may safely announce," he continued, "that private enterprise will no longer be crippled by competition with the State governments: we believe that no more canals or railroads will be undertaken by them." In short, Minor would in the future reserve his imprimatur for the private financing of railways.[4]

Poor, his successor, less a captive of the earlier image anyway, was naturally well disposed toward private enterprise and the profit motive. Within a year of taking over the *Journal*, he made his position clear in an editorial on the refusal of the Illinois legislature to allow an outside railway to cross the state. The representatives announced that they wanted to support only "internal improvements" — meaning those native to Illinois — in order to spread railroads' benefits to all their citizens. Poor scoffed and, after admitting that every "state is bound to do all it legitimately can for the promotion of the interest of its citizens," he boldly put forth the new view. "But where public works are constructed," he began his sermon, "it is impossible that all should receive the same benefit from them. . . . The works cannot run by every man's door," therefore "it is impossible but that very unequal benefits should flow from works, the burden of which come equally upon all."[5]

Once Americans accepted the premise that railways were built for the good of only some people, it was an easy step to the next proposition that the men in railroad headquarters should determine who their roads would benefit; and since many people still believed that railways symbolized the country's best traits, railroadmen in effect gained the authority to help redraft the nation's image of itself. The process proceeded with a railroad rhythm, in fits and starts. A committee of seven Philadelphia notables, for example, addressed its fellow townspeople in 1846 on behalf of the Pennsylvania Railroad and promised their railway was designed, "to enrich the Stockholders, to aid the public revenues, and to promote the large interests of an indefinitely extended commerce," presumably in that order. Granted the seven men were appealing for capital, but it still took them three more pages before they even deigned to mention the "public benefit." By the most generous interpretation, these promoters were first and foremost appealing to the public's pocketbooks.[6]

A year later President Merrick, the first to hold that office on the Pennsylvania, was far from appealing to a national unity image when he claimed that the fact that his road "must yield an immediate profit on the investment is generally admitted by all well informed persons." He thereby departed from the idealistic tone of those who only a decade earlier had maintained that railways' public service was enough to make them "profitable." Merrick was even more specific with his promise that "we may now look to capital seeking investment, and not to patriotism to furnish it." Presumably he meant local patriotism as well as national, for he was in effect announcing a corporate declaration of independence from Philadelphia, whose welfare ranked third on the committee of seven's priorities anyway. Merrick promised instead to serve the city's investment capitalists.[7]

Patterson, his successor, cleared up whatever ambiguities were left when he noted in his 1852 annual report that "it cannot be denied, that the principal object in the construction of the Pennsylvania Rail Road, was the promotion of the mercantile interests of Philadelphia." In his very next statement, he took an additional half-step toward the corporate state image when he confronted the very real possibility that his railroad might pursue goals inimical to those of the city's merchants. He reminded them that they owned much of his road's stock and promised, "I have considered it important to increase, as far as practicable, the net revenues of the road." Patterson was going to serve his constituents, not with images of the public good, but with the hard coin of the realm. With this policy he would have less reason to fear "that the mercantile interests of Philadelphia, and the pecuniary interests of the Stockholders, were incompatible with each other." The president had perceptibly narrowed the definition of his road's primary role.[8]

Poor must have been reading the Pennsylvania's annual reports, for in May 1853 he penned an editorial in which he came to remarkably similar conclusions. He began with the simple assertion that "the railroad is the agent or instrument of commerce," a notion that would have been everywhere hotly denied in the 1830s. He went on to warn that "railroads can only be built and operated at vast cost, and if we anticipate the wants of a community in construction, or build them where they are not needed, the most disastrous results cannot fail to follow." The railways' ability to attract increasing traffic, he thought, was the key to prosperity. As early as 1851 President Patterson showed he knew how companies lured that new business; it was through "the knowledge and practice by their managers, of the laws which develop sources of revenue, and give animation to the business of the improvements committed to their charge."[9]

As railway officials used this knowledge to increase their power within their individual companies, their excesses grew in proportion. Too many executives in the East began to operate in secret, resort to shady financial practices and schemes, engage in unhealthy speculation that occasionally bordered upon outright fraud, and encourage corporate rivalries that redounded to everyone's detriment. In the process, railroads shed the last remnants of their former image as promoters of the public good, and it was another two generations before they attracted anything other than a hostile press.

Secrecy in railway headquarters upset many outside industry ob-

Tunnels such as this one finished before the Civil War
through Missionary Ridge in Chattanooga, Tennessee,
"shortened distances" and attracted traffic.
(Photo by Richard Jackson)

servers. In 1853, for example, Poor tried to reverse the trend toward secrecy in corporate affairs, warning that only men intent upon doing evil would resort to maneuvering behind the scenes. And he fully understood what such actions would do to their reputations when he preached to his readers that when "directors of roads are silent both as to their plans and their mode of executing them, they have no pledges before the public to be fulfilled, with the penalty of loss of character and position in case of failure." In such cases — and here Poor was specifically referring to the Erie Railroad, already well on its way to becoming the *bête noire* of the industry — Poor feared "the enterprise is left to take care of itself, or to the care of those who will only use it for their own advantage." The real danger he thought was "the public taking it for granted, that from the respectability of the names of the directors the enterprise is properly conducted." The editor understood that interweaving personal affairs with the public's business conducted in private led to the public's loss of control over corporate actions. Poor had witnessed an actual case of this back in 1851 when Congress appropriated 2.5 million acres of land for the Illinois Central Railroad. The New Yorker had supported the bill, despite the fact that he had the sinking feeling that "the bounty of Congress will inure, as it generally does, to those who have wealth to control its direction." After the legislation was passed, he was sure that was what had happened, although he could not prove it. All he could do was to lament publicly, "we will confess, that our cooperation to this end would have by no means been so hearty, had we foreseen that it would probably conduce much more to private aggrandizement, than to public good."[10]

Poor felt strongly about railroads conducting their business openly, for he had long feared that otherwise their treasuries would be too great a temptation for officials to resist. He made a general statement on corporate honesty as early as 1849, when he pointed out that "the motives brought to bear upon the Directors, and the careful scrutiny exercised by the whole community over all their acts, are the best pledges that can be given for the honest discharge of their duties." He admitted that "they make mistakes," but under the harsh glare of publicity, "they will not sacrifice the interests of the roads for selfish purposes." The slight whiff of railway corruption was already swirling about the New York City financial districts, and Minor was moved to issue a warning that year. He was stunned by the large amalgamations in Great Britain which had created a corporate monster the editor claimed would be capitalized at more than $200 million. He was afraid something of the sort might happen in the United States and advised against it because "those who may be entrusted with its management *may possibly*, in the consciousness of their own power, forget the rights of others, and become too strong for the government itself."[11]

The nineteenth-century equivalent of multinational firms was the transcontinental, a scheme so big that many Americans could not even imagine its scope. Poor could, however and, looking into his crystal ball, cautioned that the gargantuan sums it involved would prove too tempting for its promoters. He especially did not like Asa Whitney's proposal to build the road as a private venture if the government would grant him personally a large amount of free land to use for financing it. The New York editor's comments in 1849 pointed up the transition in image that was just getting underway when he forewarned that "the rights of all our citizens, and the commerce of the world, should never be surrendered to the management of individuals who might have no other principle of action than their own cupidity, and," he emphasized, "whose interest would come in direct conflict with that of the public." Instead, Poor proposed that the government should build the transcontinental and operate it through a congressionally appointed board of directors composed of one representative from each state. He was certainly not against private ownership, he just wanted to relieve as far as possible "all fear of abuse or mismanagement of power either by the private individuals or corrupt officials."[12]

Great fortunes could also be made quickly from the railroad industry without resorting to internal corporate chicanery. The business spawned an unintentional byproduct: stock speculations on an unheard of scale, in which daring promoters could get rich, sometimes even at the expense of their own roads' fiscal health. Speculation, of course, was much older than the railway business, but as the number of rail offerings increased and capitalizations did likewise, the number of gamblers attracted to the sport similarly rose. By mid-century, as the stakes grew and the game became proportionally more risky, speculators moved into railway offices all over the country to attempt to manipulate railroad policies for their own benefits. With corporate strategies increasingly plotted behind closed doors, it became difficult to ascribe motivations to railroad officials' actions; the public, under a barrage of constant accusations of corporate peculation, began to suspect all railroad officers. The wedge was driven ever deeper between the images of railroads as devices for serving the public's interest and as vehicles for private gain. Increasingly, American railway leaders, like national rulers, were pictured as flaunting their riches while they sketched the political and economic policies within their purview with the intent of augmenting their personal power and fortune. Too numerous specific instances of widespread speculation in corporate front offices further fleshed in the emerging corporate state image in both the minds of the public and in actuality.

Initially, the gravest charge that could be leveled against speculators was that their machinations with volatile "fancy stocks" kept all stock prices abnormally low, thereby depriving promoters of the capital they so desperately needed. Minor, who bragged that since he did not own a share of railroad stock he could remain impartial (although his constant pleas to subscribers to pay their bills hint that he could not *afford* to buy securities), first attacked the "stock jobbers" in the depths of the depression. He complained that "while 'fancy stocks,' are continually noticed at every sale—the best railroad stocks are seldom heard of, and in proportion to their value as investments, are kept from the public notice." The unfortunate consequence, he thought, was "that in general notoriety is attached only to those works which either from being remarkable failures, or from some other cause have become a sort of foot ball among brokers." To advertise more substantial offerings, the Boston *Courier* published a list of local railway shares in 1847 and pointedly assured its readers that "these solid securities are like gold dust in the market"—a claim that must have brought a glint to the eye of every speculator on the East Coast.[13]

Poor disliked speculators as a caste, and in an early editorial he warned that they could gain control of roads and use their professional tricks to keep their stock prices artificially high. Less than three years later his prediction came true; Poor awoke to the fact that speculators had moved into the front offices of the Erie Railroad. Undoubtedly his pique over this realization was intensified by the fact that he and Minor had long compaigned for construction of that road, and he took some deserved responsibility for it. So he bore down hard on the company's officers in June 1852 for declaring what he considered was an unearned dividend. Competition, he argued, had reduced rates "to produce an income only sufficient to pay a fair dividend" upon the road's cost while the announced payoff was forced by outside pressure. And he knew just who applied it: "vast quantities of the stock is [*sic*] carried by speculators in the street," he noted ominously. A year later Poor announced with undisguised glee that the road's treasurer had either quit or been fired. The editor believed the man "has enjoyed the reputation of being the leading speculator in the stock and securities of the company." The treasurer's resignation did not end the corporate mischief, for in the fall of 1853 Poor was lecturing Erie officials again. Finally, almost in desperation, he concluded "the Erie has always been a *nest* for speculators."[14]

The barrage of articles detailing railway speculations made Americans increasingly nervous about any rail consolidation that would increase the power of railway officers and give them even more securities to play with. On the eve of the mergers that created the New York Central in 1853, Poor sought to allay such fears with the upbeat thought that "the friends of the railroad system in this country may well congratulate themselves that there is as little tendency towards centralizing preponderance of control in the various parts of the grand machine of its commerce, as there is in the working of the political affairs of the country." That he truly believed his assertion was somewhat suspect, especially after he undercut his own contentions later in the same editorial, confessing "we admit the power of wealth and its tendency to concentration." He sought to explain the apparent contradiction by noting that all a railroad manager looks for "is a profitable investment, and utterly shrinks from the exercise of any further control as an unpaid gratuitous labor." Poor was still just groping toward the political imagery that was gradually developing around his railroad world; in the early 1850s, however, the outlines of the corporate state image were still fuzzy.[15]

When the New York legislature debated the New York Central's charter the following spring, Poor favored its passage, claiming that "the economy of the thing was the first argument for consolidation." Although he was well aware of the principal "objection to it, the monopoly it would have a tendency to create," he stuck to his guns and defended the mergers with the promise that "we do not see any danger of excessive charges, nor in fact of a management of which the public will have a right to complain." He was still persuaded that large works in the hands of good men were in the natural order of things, while big companies in the hands of evil speculators were an economic aberration that should be exposed to the full glare of publicity and remedied. He hoped that the consolidated roads would serve the public good just as the smaller lines had done, but he was anything but certain that would be the case.[16]

As railroad companies all over the East became larger, their officers soon found that the competitive pressures they faced became more severe. They were ensnared in a vicious cycle; the bigger their railroads grew, the greater the pressures on them to protect their traffic through more consolidations. Rivalries everywhere became sharper, ushering in metaphors of corporate feudalism at headquarters all over the East. Herman Haupt, the superintendent of transportation on the Pennsylvania Railroad, for example, worried in 1852 about the other eastern trunk lines cutting his road off from the western trade. When he pressed his fears on his boss, President Thomson, Haupt reached back five centuries for a metaphor; he warned that "the difficulty of any competition with these lines at this time is very great and we may not be able *to enter the lists* as successful competitors until next year."

If company officials viewed competition as a matter every bit as serious as the fourteenth-century joust, Poor demonstrated his own naiveté a few months later when he took up the general subject again. Somewhere he picked up his premise that roads twenty-five miles or more apart were not really competitors. From there he went on to twit rail managers that it was "folly to run prices down so low as to make both unprofitable by allowing the loss on any through business to eat up the profits on local." Haupt must have chuckled when he read the editorial, for he was fighting the Erie railroad located hundreds of miles to the north.[17]

The eastern railroad managers first considered reaction to the increasingly bitter rivalry was to work out their differences cooperatively in harmony with the old unity image or, as Haupt put it, to carry on "negotiations." Although an initial meeting to relieve competitive irritants in the East took place as early as 1851, the first to reach the public prints convened at Springfield, Massachusetts, in October 1852 to consider establishing common rates and procedures and to discuss patent problems. Its results, though inconclusive, were encouraging enough that a larger group of officials met a month later in the same city. At that gathering, rail managers made it perfectly clear to the press that they were meeting because "in the opinion of this convention the value of railroad stock would be much enhanced, and dividends increased, by a more harmonious action and friendly co-operation among all the lines of railways throughout the country." Twenty years earlier any promoter who ventured such sentiments would have been fired.[18]

Apparently pleased with the results of their two meetings that fall, railroad officers promised to reconvene seven months later at Saratoga to reconfirm cooperative arrangements. The New England managers could not wait that long, however, and in mid-January 1853 met in Boston, where they unanimously agreed to request the roads in that region to advance their freight tariffs immediately a full 25 percent and to stop issuing free passes. The first two or three meetings set the tone for the remainder of the decade. Railway managers, even while they paid lip service to the laws of trade, desperately sought a community of interests that would enable them to stabilize their competitive situations, raise their rates as high as possible, cut out free passes, and pool the business at busy points. They were most candid about why they were meeting; in 1859 Thomson informed his stockholders that the presidents of the middle Atlantic trunk lines met to effect "a harmony of purpose conducive to the mutual advantage of the railway interest and the public." His ordering of priorities indicated how far the old national unity image had fallen into disfavor. The railway executives' image of their place in society perceptibly narrowed to concentrate on their immediate corporate prosperity and survival. If such goals served the public interest, and probably most thought there was an intimate connection between the two, then all was well and good. If their private interests did not coincide with the public's, officials knew which they had to serve.[19]

Railway development in the last half of the nineteenth century would have been profoundly different had attempts to cooperate succeeded. Instead, railroad executives dropped all pretense to the gentlemanly conduct of business in the national interest and, like the nation's politicians, sought to defend their particular interests. An industry leader such as Thomson was doing so when he wrote his counterpart John Work Garrett on the B&O that "we neither stoop to get trade by unfair means, or poach upon our neighbors grounds." That Garrett viewed the world the same way was clear when he wrote Charles Moran, president of the Erie, that the B&O did not object to anything Moran did for his road's local interests as long as it "is necessary for your protection."[20]

War was the ultimate means of protecting one's interests, and railroad managers became masters at the art long before their political counterparts. Railroad correspondence reeked with war talk as the rate-cutting bouts threatened everyone's fiscal health. In the middle of one such contest in the summer of 1859, Thomson wrote Garrett a curt note advising him "we must drop the whole subject —And fight on." Out in the Midwest, Samuel Barlow of the Ohio and Mississippi, a road that was constantly whipsawed by eastern rate wars, wrote Garrett that his feeble efforts to mediate were "better than to continue the present warfare." As railway managers in the East become more sophisticated, they chose up sides in their wars. Thomson warned the B&O that it had better join with the Pennsylvania "or the Southern lines will be at war with one another instead of presenting a united front to our Northern Rivals." A day later, he threatened that if Garrett refused to come to terms "and prefer[ed] to war with this company," then the Keystone road "will make any requisite sacrifices to maintain correct principles and preserve its permanent interests." Other wars were already raging; Thomson told Garrett that Erastus Corning on the New York Central "is in fact, in a war with the canal."[21]

Railroad managers laid up a veritable linguistic arsenal to deal with the hostile world in which they lived. Garrett, for example, once assured Thomson that "I would regard it as mere weakness to abandon important interests." While Barlow, as usual ruing the impossibility of getting all the warring parties to observe an earlier agreement, complained to Garrett that "if any of them find they cannot submit to work under it, they may break up the whole thing and open the fight." In 1860 with the presidential canvass in full fury, Garrett accused Thomson of breaking rate pacts, to which the Pennsylvania's president replied to a B&O underling, "I would suggest to your president that it is neither neighborly or wise on his part to be interfering in family quarrels"—the family metaphor was a two-edged weapon.[22]

Officials were well versed in the language of conflict and warfare by the Civil War, but one of the great ironies of that period was that once the nation was torn asunder and war was on everyone's tongue, railway managers dropped the war metaphors and declared peace in their business world. National unity took on new and poignant meanings during the war and for the first time became a practical rather than an idealistic question. And equally important, wartime demands brought enough traffic to tax the capacity of all the eastern trunk lines. By the following year in fact, railway managers quarreled more with the government than among themselves. Federal contracts in the North enabled many roads to earn extraordinary profits and served the same purpose as the prewar agreements; they stipulated maximum rates, distances, and to some degree pooled traffic among the eastern lines.

Railway leaders certainly had not foreseen the effects their images and actions would have; they were probably the most surprised people in the nation when cannonballs arced over Charleston's harbor. Almost to a man they decried the stupidity of breaking up the Union and destroying the mutually compatible commercial relations that existed between the slave and free states. Naturally, officials on those lines that ran north-south, such as the Louisville and Nashville or the Illinois Central, and those on the larger border state roads such as the B&O, which traversed both slave and free territory, were terrified by the prospects of war. Like all men of business, railroaders sought stability and regularity in their commercial affairs, and a civil war promised neither.

The irony of all this was, however, that the rail industry, for thirty years the great hope for permanent peace, prosperity, and national unity, proved more important in war. Virtually all the literature on Civil War railroads indicates that northern roads, with their superior facilities, enabled the Union to construct, maintain, and supply a vastly superior war machine that eventually wore down the Confederate forces. Moreover, commanders on both sides changed their traditional strategies; rail junctions suddenly became important military goals as the great battles at Cornith, Chattanooga, and Atlanta testify. Troops were routed along railroads both for purposes of transport and when they moved on foot to take advantage of a level roadbed and bridges over the water courses. More fundamentally, commanders knew that if their men stuck to nearby rail lines they were much less likely to get lost.

The war dramatically sped up changes already underway on American railways; everywhere railroad managers solidified and enhanced their positions in national life. Many railroads made a great deal of money during the war; cash dividends of over 10 percent per year were not uncommon. Although much of their prosperity was a direct outgrowth of inflation, most roads emerged from the war in much strengthened financial positions that enabled them to improve, enlarge, and update their physical plants. The men who guided their destinies during the conflict became important political figures, as they were often consulted before armies moved and on general political and military business. At war's end, the men who controlled the nation's largest businesses, flush with newly found wealth and political influence, sought to secure their peacetime economic positions and to retain the traffic they had gained during the conflict. With bulging treasuries and gilt-edged credit, they sought security through expansion. The completion of the first transcontinental railroad in 1869, America's real symbol of unity, widened their horizons. The stakes in the business had been raised, and a whole postwar generation of railway leaders, nurtured on the corporate state image and the metaphors of hostility both in their offices and on the field of battle, were poised to exploit any opportunities. They extended the new image to its limit and acted in accordance with it. In so doing, they wrote a chapter in their nation's history that distinguished it from most other industrial nations, and created what Thomas Cochran has most aptly called, "The Legend of the Robber Barons."[23]

CHAPTER 12

The Problems of Empire

|—|—|—|—|—|—|—|—|—|—|—|—|—|—|—|—|

I n his book, *The Entrepreneurs*, Robert Sobel tells a story about Edward H. Harriman's audience with Emperor Franz Joseph of Austria-Hungary. His Highness was late for the appointment and, after a functionary explained the delay to Harriman, the railroad owner airily replied, "I, of all people, know the problems of empire." Although the story is probably apocryphal, contemporary Americans would not have found the diminutive Harriman's response odd. After the Civil War, men of business, commanding undreamed-of riches — people such as Harriman, J.P. Morgan , Jim Fisk, Jay Gould, Commodore and his son William Vanderbilt, Collis P. Huntington and his California colleagues, Andrew Carnegie, and Thomas A. Scott — dominated thousands of miles of major railroad properties. Americans had never seen anybody quite like them. They appeared to break with long-established commercial traditions, to defy conventional norms of morality, and to display an arrogance usually associated only with royalty. [1]

Those attributes, however, were a natural outgrowth of the extension of the prewar corporate state image. That notion converged with larger currents reshaping the character of postwar America to magnify developments in the railway business. The Union's victory accelerated the transfer of political power from the states to Washington, D.C., a trend that was already apparent before the conflict. At the same time state governments, responsible for the conduct of corporations created within their borders, were less willing, and in some cases unable, to control their corporate progeny. In states such as Pennsylvania and California, in fact, railroad interests gained at least a de facto veto over legislation. The federal government evinced little interest for twenty years after the war in controlling corporations. Left to their own devices, railway leaders and others pursued their interests in harmony with their self-image. In the postwar period that image bore a striking resemblance to the larger American impetus toward fashioning a stronger nation-state. At least until the mid-1870s railway developments paralleled the basic changes taking place in the character of America.

Railroad owners and managers were among the most important men of that generation. As Alfred D. Chandler, Jr., has suggested, these men controlled huge new business agglomerations that were the first "to work out the modern ways of finance, management, labor relations, competition, and government regulation" that shaped the lives of later generations.[2] The power of their immense capital resources demanded public respect for their views and authority; what they thought of themselves and of their places in society became of great moment to all Americans. The fortunes they amassed, the lives they controlled, the political influence they wielded, and the awe they inspired speeded up the process of centralization in America.

In trying to shape their world to conform to their image, however, railway leaders irrevocably changed the face of America, and initially at a pace too rapid to allow the formation of the mental concepts necessary to make the new world they brought intelligible. Charles Elliott Perkins, president of the Chicago, Burlington and Quincy, recognized this point in 1884 when he warned an associate, "the spirit of the age is communistic, perhaps because the progress of civilization has developed more rapidly than it has *disciplined* the sympathies of people."[3] The mood Perkins complained of, however, was the product of a mental representation of reality that prompted Harriman's response.

Postwar railroad executives consolidated many of the corporate entities dotting the Balkanized railway map and formed huge railroad systems that stretched from the Atlantic Seaboard to the Mississippi River and from there to the West Coast. These trunk lines were giant, powerful companies, locked in a titanic struggle with each other for control of through traffic. Some spanned half a continent, were tightly organized, commanded assets far in excess of the United States Treasury, daily risked their great fortunes, and always feared proportionally huge losses. Corporate self-interest was the principal mainspring for their actions, profit and loss the barometer of their success or failure. Railway managers, not surprisingly, began to see themselves as sovereign rulers wielding vast authority over their corporate domains while beset by predators on all sides. That generation's officers absorbed the rhetoric, posturing, and political emphasis of their age, and took the flavor of such strong, often vitriolic language to their offices, where they used it to point up the analogy between their corporate situations and that of the nation. The Civil War, with its four long years of bloody news from various fronts, with its glorification of the manly virtues of force and fury, only served to gild the language of corporate executives with strong, vivid, and often gory metaphors.

The men who ruled railroad empires after the war competed with the perfervid oratory of the Reconstruction Era to provide a major part of the period's color. Because they thought and functioned like national officials, they adopted the language of statecraft. Corporate officers delivered "ultimatums," declared their "neutrality" on certain issues, went on the defensive to protect their "territory," and sued for "peace" when no other recourse was available. Like their counterparts in the political arena, railway leaders knew how to wreak violence, both financial and linguistic, to attain their ends. They were masters at the art of verbal assault, thrashing each other metaphorically, strewing verbal carnage everywhere. Competitors became "enemies" and sometimes "pirates." Railway forces mounted "attacks" or launched "incursions" to gain "spoils" or even "indemnities." Businessmen negotiated "alliances" to obtain "allies" before setting out to "fight" a "war." They sought to "slaughter" or "destroy" their opponents on the field of "battle" in order to obtain a "victory" and a favorable "treaty." From their own letters, newspaper reports, and the general literature of the time, one cannot imagine a more belligerent lot of properly attired, usually rational, more often than not respected upper-class gentlemen. Only in such a metaphorical context can Harriman's reputed remark in Vienna be seen as anything other than the vainglorious boast of a parvenu.

These men did not live in a make-believe world. Their self-image, like all viable images, had a convincing factual basis; the analogy between the mature railroad corporation and the United States, for example, while not all-encompassing, was striking enough. Both operated under documents from which they derived their legitimacy and authority. These documents were drawn and empowered by legally sanctioned bodies, the Constitutional Convention and the state legislatures, and included amending processes. The charters conferred upon their respective holders certain rights, powers, and duties and acknowledged forms of higher law, in the one case natural law and in the other the laws of trade and commerce. These unwritten laws provided additional legitimacy from recognized authorities who overarched the mundane legal process and enabled officials operating under each to appeal to a higher reason. Moreover, in keeping with the constitutional experience, the limits of corporate power were not rigidly defined, but over the three decades prior to the Civil War railway officers slowly clarified the lines of authority.[4]

Although early legislators did not anticipate that railroad companies would assume identities of their own, by the 1850s some lines had become as organic and self-conscious of their own destinies as the states that created them. But even in their independent developments, they remained politically analogous to nation-states. On the New York Central, Erie, Pennsylvania, and Baltimore & Ohio — the so-called Big Four roads of the East — managerial organizations in the 1870s ranged from the autocratic to semi-democratic. William H. Vanderbilt, who inherited majority control of the New York Central from his father, ruled, if not like a divine-right king, then at least with the powers of a Franz Joseph; while Hugh J. Jewett, a lawyer by profession and a politician by aspiration, presided over his road in the traditions of both and rode the Erie into bankruptcy in 1875, only to emerge as its court-appointed receiver. Thomas A. Scott, the handsome paragon of Sidney Hook's man of action and a born charmer, picked up the Pennsylvania's presidential reins in 1874 after the death of the staid Thomson and maintained a hesitant accountability to his restive stockholders through the remainder of the depression. Farther south, Garrett, who had been chosen president of the Baltimore & Ohio in 1858 by Johns Hopkins, the road's largest stockholder, guided the destinies of the line with a slow, sure hand. By the late 1870s, however, Garrett was treading the path to corporate autocracy, having earlier been one of the more "democratic" presidents. Like the rest of the globe, the railway world was dotted with a bewildering diversity of political systems, all struggling to coexist.

Railway leaders, however, recognized that the corporate state analogy was much more extensive than simple political comparisons would suggest. In common with heads of state, they defined their business domains in terms of people and territory. Each company had its own "nationals"—people dependent upon the railway for their livelihood and security. To one degree or another, employees, agents, shippers, suppliers, politicians, bankers, merchants, and newspaper editors considered themselves "Central" men, "Pennsy" men, or whatever, and adopted the corporate images shaped in the front offices. If their public image differed from the company's, they faced the potential charge of "disloyalty" and the threat of termination. Railway executives placed a high premium on loyalty and often spent heavily to buy or manufacture it. Moreover, they assumed that anyone disloyal was unlikely to become a trusted compatriot on another road, and so they maintained blacklists that practically insured permanent expatriation for anybody so proscribed.

The concept of loyalty was tightly interwoven with a military analogy that often invaded the correspondence of railroad men. Indeed, the very conditions of railway employment prompted an inevitable comparison with the army. Workers, especially the unskilled, were paid low wages, liable for stints of long hours on the job, especially in times of man-made or natural disasters, subject to severe discipline, graded according to rank, and required to perform dangerous tasks. The minutes of many boards of directors attest to the frequency with which workers were killed or maimed in the line of duty—it was an acknowledged part of the job. Moreover, any pretense of corporate democracy stopped at the level of superintendent. Below that rank, companies established rigid chains of command to coordinate the efforts of thousands of employees strung out over hundreds of miles of track.

Chandler recognized the analogy to the army, noting that labor and management "became separated by barriers almost as formidable as those between the officer and enlisted man in the military service." Contemporary observers saw it as well. In the 1870s Perkins complained of the haphazard organization on his Burlington, explaining that "the Vice-President and the Auditor are generals not having anything to do with the regimental organization. The working organization of a Railroad, *the daily machine, so to speak*, may I think be modeled on that of the Army, the Co. being the unit!" Nearby, the Chicago and Northwestern's vice president, M.L. Sykes, was driven to a like metaphor after Jay Gould had smashed the Iowa Pool; he recommended caution, waiting with "sentinels posted but with instructions not to make an engagement with the enemy." Corporate military personnel were cheaply secured in the 1870s; until the labor outburst of 1877, railway officials considered company soldiers simply another commodity to be purchased on the open market in accordance with the laws of trade and commerce.[5]

Territory, another prime component of the corporate state image, was a much more complicated matter. That concept, which went to the very heart of the railroad leaders' image, evoked the strongest metaphorical outbursts. Few men, however, were as direct as John Murray Forbes, who owned a large interest in the Burlington, and who accused the Northwestern of invading "our country," or Perkins who described the Burlington and Missouri River Railroad in Nebraska as "a sovereign power," or a Burlington official who charged that officers on the Rock Island acted as if they "owned the earth." But control of territory with a captive trade that could be charged monopolistic tariffs provided companies a desperately sought measure of fiscal protection. For if prosperity, survival, and security were the most important aims of all nation-states and railroads, they could be advanced most easily in the world of transport through mastery of local traffic; in good times that trade often met the basic corporate budget obligations.[6]

In the three decades following 1857, however, a time in which rates fell relentlessly due to fierce competition and the postwar deflation, local revenues met railway managers' needs less often. More-over, on the older eastern roads, officers were no longer able to squeeze additional profits from internal economies; they had already spent years streamlining their organizational structures. They therefore looked to the growing through-traffic for their salvation, but that trade, by definition, crossed territorial borders, necessitating cooperation with frequently hostile neighbors or a policy of aggressive territorial expansion. By the postwar period most leaders learned that the most secure strategy to capture a greater portion of the through trade was to control the routes. This discovery dovetailed very neatly with their new image; they could justify enlarging their territorial boundaries as a means of defending their vital interests.

It was only later, certainly by the late 1870s, that railway leaders saw the fallacy inherent in their territorial strategies. As they expanded, they had to defend a greater area either from older rivals who had become larger and more powerful, or from new competitors who had once been neutral or had not figured in diplomatic calculations. Once started there was no stopping; their roads had to expand or die. Maury Klein noted over a decade ago in his article on postwar southern railway strategists that "expansion continued because railway managers perceived it as a necessity for survival . . . without it the company would die of atrophy." Contemporary railroad men would have agreed. J. Edgar Thomson never tired of telling anyone who would listen that "we cannot stand still for that means slipping back, we must constantly go forward." James Joy, an excitable Boston financier who always stood ready to add to his already extensive holdings in the Midwest, showed that he also understood the necessity for territorial expansion — and the consequences of failure — when he wrote "I know nothing which in my opinion would be so unwise as for us to fold our hands and allow rival enterprises to occupy our domains . . . if we mean to maintain ourselves and command the business of the country."[7]

Railway executives sought to fill their treasuries and secure the prosperity of their roads by beggaring their neighbors. Their techniques differed very little from those of the imperial nations; railroad officials tried to "colonize" adjacent territories through the lease or purchase of conveniently situated weaker roads that could se-

Locomotives that bordered on being works of art
claimed and held territories for railways.
(*Poor's Manual, 1889*)

cure a useful trade for the mother line. These consolidations augmented the earnings of the stronger roads, denied that locality's traffic to rivals, and lessened competition in the immediate area. As Julius Grodinsky noted in his *Transcontinental Railway Strategy*, these actions secured "the grand objective . . . an entrenched position."[8]

To survive, railroadmen immersed themselves in balance-of-power corporate diplomacy and freely adopted its parlance. John King, vice president of the B&O, reported to Garrett in 1875 that the Erie believed "the Penna & Balt. & Ohio had made an alliance to fight the Northern lines." Often railway managers became very formal — Garrett suggested in 1878 that his road "make a treaty" with Vanderbilt. Newspaper reporters also picked up diplomatic analogies, although this sometimes created problems for the lines. Scott once had to write Garrett to deny a press report that he "had entered into a combination Saturday offensive and defensive against your Road." Officials out in the trans-Mississippi West also understood diplomatic rhetoric. John F. Tracey, who controlled the Northwestern, suggested that his road, the Rock Island, and the Burlington unite "in an alliance offensive if need be, and defensive at all events for this business." In the heady days of the early 1870s, Joy wrote to John Newell, president of the Illinois Central, claiming that he wished to "make a perpetual treaty of alliance to work together" with the Northwestern so that "we have a friend and ally, instead of a rival." Failing to make alliances, railroad diplomats resorted to the refuge of all careful statesmen; Forbes, after discovering that he could not break "the grasping monopoly" of the Union Pacific, decided that the best policy was "maintenance of the 'status quo.'" And back east, King, in the midst of a particularly vicious rate war, rued the fact that Scott was not yet "prepared for 'status quo ante bellum'" because, King continued, it would be "too humiliating for him to adopt it now."[9]

Railway leaders did more than use the rhetoric of diplomacy — their actions corresponded to the image that gave rise to such language. Like the corporate statesmen they envisioned themselves to be, they avidly sought to tip the balances of power in their favor, keeping in mind the crucial differences between long- and short-term advantages to be gained from tactical maneuvers. In efforts to protect their capital and squeeze the last bit of traffic from their opponents, they forged remarkably long-lasting alliances with natural allies, made temporary agreements with others when expedient, and ruthlessly disrupted the trade of their competitors. The more dismal the national economy and the more precarious the company ledgers, the more furiously the corporate diplomats maneuvered.

For all the conflict in the railroad world after the Civil War, industry leaders, like their national counterparts, steadfastly averred that they abhorred corporate wars. The record bears them out. Railway officials usually sought to achieve their aims short of war, even as they metaphorically postured, bluffed, cajoled, and threatened in an effort to lure that last ton of traffic over their lines. With constantly rising levels of capital investment, large numbers of employees that had to be paid regardless of the tonnage hauled, and staggering annual interest obligations, corporate executives needed to be aggressive. But they escalated their rhetoric with care in an attempt to avoid the very conflicts they threatened.

Railway leaders became quite adept at finding means of intimidating each other without precipitating open hostilities. An effective ploy was to threaten a rival at the lower corporate ranks, as when Garrett's general freight agent told Alexander J. Cassatt, the third vice president of the Pennsylvania, that the B&O was considering a connection with the Pittsburgh and Lake Erie. Cassatt "professed very great dissatisfaction," agent Smith reported, "and threatened war on B&O revenue etc. etc.," but it was essentially a harmless outburst. Or a vice president could try to intimidate the president of a rival road, the disparity in ranks taking some of the sting out of the message, as when the Pennsylvania's vice president George B. Roberts, warned Garrett that "the efforts of your company to disturb the friendly relations now existing between us" were not appreciated.[10]

The metaphorical continuum from verbal abuse to overt action, however, was a small but carefully graduated one. In 1877, embroiled in a dispute with Standard Oil and the other trunk lines and with no oil moving to Baltimore, King accused the oil firm of having an "apparent design especially to be hostile and unjust to the Baltimore & Ohio Company." President William K. Ackerman of the

Illinois Central understood the intermediate nature of hostile as metaphor and further illustrated that the accepted rhetoric knew no geographical bounds. Commenting to a company director in 1878 about Burlington aggressions against his road, Ackerman complained that they were "both unbusinesslike and unfriendly" and professed amazed disbelief that "they would array themselves in open hostility to us." "Open hostility" was very close to a euphemism for war and was meant to be so. The next step was to drop all pretense to such niceties as Garrett did when he wrote Scott despondently in 1877 that "wasteful battles are made against the interests we all represent. The public are literally sickened with these continuous hostilities and unending contests. With war about petroleum and war about passengers there will soon be little hope of maintaining peace." Garrett's concern with keeping the peace in the midst of wars pointed up the truth of Charles Francis Adams's wry comment that, with the railway executive of the 1870s, peace "is always a condition of semi-warfare."[11]

Corporate wars, the diplomacy of last resort, were a primary source of much of the era's metaphorical color. When the rate structure collapsed in 1875, King complained to Garrett that the Pennsylvania had launched an "unspeakable and unprovoked attack on our freight business." Four years later the B&O's directors claimed that they had been under the mistaken belief that their contract had rendered them "safe from the aggressions of the Pennsylvania Railroad Company." Sometimes railway leaders consciously sought to be aggressive. President John W. Brooks sketched out such a policy for the chief engineer of the Burlington and Missouri River in Nebraska, although he warned the officer to keep "the Co. out of sight as much as possible" as their efforts "would be weakened by the Company appearing to be the aggressor." It was always diplomatic to deny aggressive intent even when it was obvious to all. In 1880 Forbes patiently explained to a Rock Island official that his takeover of the above Nebraska road "is not aggressive toward Rock Island, but is really a peace measure for all." Railway leaders expected each other to be aggressive; their image demanded it. The sigh of relief was almost audible when Frederick J. Kimball wrote a director on his Norfolk & Western in 1885, "fortunately for us, the C.&O. people are not very active or aggressive."[12]

The Chesapeake men were rarities in the postwar railroad world. Letters of the period were full of warnings that war was about to break out, news that it was already raging, or hope that it was about to end. In the East, where wars usually upset the precarious equilibrium of other regional balances, conflicts were not only frequent but, as Garrett pointed out, selective. Wars over grain, oil, livestock, and passengers often overlapped rate disputes at various shipping points, problems with car supply, and fights over connections, rebates, express companies, and agents. These conflicts always seemed to raise the adrenalin of railway leaders. In early 1874 King wrote Garrett that "our passenger war turned out to be the most exciting matter that has happened in regard to railroad affairs for a long time," and he observed that business had risen sharply on the B&O due to the drastic rate cuts. Continuing the metaphor he added, "our opponent was very much ridiculed and our cause considerably strengthened." Six months later King still took pride in the B&O's victory when he wrote that "the loss of prestige resulting from their defeat in the recent war has been very great." And he was already preparing for the next conflict. Complaining to Garrett that the Pennsylvania's transfer costs for B&O cars were too high, he suggested "the Point Look Out road is a good rod to hold over the Penn. Co."[13]

When given a reasonable chance to gain some strategic object worth fighting for, railway officials threw aside all caution. In the process, their hostile language mirrored that of their political counterparts. In Iowa, for example, Perkins warned officials on the Rock Island that if they persisted in building a branch road, the Burlington would consider it a "declaration of war." From Congress in 1876, where Collis P. Huntington of the Southern Pacific was waging the fight to stop Scott's Texas and Pacific from building across the Southwest, he wrote his associate Charles Colton of his upcoming meeting: "I expect to see him [Scott] on the 26th and then I will know if we are to have war or peace and will let you know." Ackerman, in 1881, seemed very casual about it all, "I think we can indulge in one small railroad war," he wrote a director. The following year, however, he was not so sanguine. "The fury of this warfare must expend itself," he explained with a trace of edginess to a vice president of the Wabash, "before Managers can reason soberly." A little over a decade earlier John Henry Devereux, veteran of service with the United States Military Railroads and general manager of the Lake Shore & Michigan Southern, wrote his president, Horace Clark, Vanderbilt's son-in-law, "you have not a man I believe who will not gird his loins afresh to do battle mightily, that the increased facilities you have given us may be used to the utmost." Not all industry leaders allowed emotion and rhetoric to overcome reason; Robert Harris, president of the Burlington, once told former vice president of the United States Schuyler Colfax that in business matters he subscribed to what he called a "military maxim" that went:

> He who fights and runs away
> Lives to fight another day.[14]

The more expressive railway leaders also employed metaphorical weaponry in their corporate wars. Ackerman boasted in 1881 for example, that "our guns once aimed at the Chicago and Eastern Illinois would soon bring them to terms." The same metaphor appealed to Frederick Billings when he wrote Henry Villard asking "why, virtually, put a pistol at the breast of the Northern Pacific at Ainsworth or Wallula, and say this far and no further?" The superintendent of the Council Bluffs road in Iowa complained that the Burlington in Nebraska, by running its cars into the Union Pacific depot at Omaha, had "opened its batteries" on his road. Not all railroadmen used the latest military technology in their metaphors. In 1875 one official on the Northwestern predicted that if the Rock Island acquired a line to Rockford, Illinois, it would "send a javelin" into the side of the Northwestern. On a more literal plane, the treasurer of the Gatling Gun Company wrote Garrett after the 1877 riots that "one Gatling, with a full supply of ammunition, can clear a street or track, and keep it clear." Garrett's reply has been lost, but it seems reasonable to assume that, like his peers, he felt more comfortable remaining metaphorical.[15]

The metaphor of weaponry naturally led railway leaders to express their situations in terms of the destruction and carnage violence wrought. Most executives employed only general terms. Ackerman once accused an enemy of having "inflicted great injury upon our traffic for the past three years." John Griswold, a Burlington director, advised Perkins in 1884 that "if we fight and hurt the M.P.

Railroad empires were built on the profits earned
by homely little freight cars such as this wooden gondola.
(*Poor's Manual, 1889*)

[Missouri Pacific] we shall be worse off with a bankrupt road along side of us than with a solvent one." While addressing the Convention of Southern Railroad and Steamship Lines, Herman Haupt, a graduate of West Point and a veteran of the Civil War, explained that rate wars "inflict serious injury upon all competitors." In 1879 the B&O's board accused the Pennsylvania of acting "with the determination of doing the greatest possible injury to the interests of this Company." Albert Fink's brother Henry remarked in 1905 that rate cutting led to "injury" and could lead to "riots and bloodshed," although in hindsight we know he was not speaking entirely metaphorically. Joy had no such advantage back in 1854 when he contended the Illinois Central had "used its power to crush and destroy the prosperity of a city of its own state." The rate fights of 1874, precipitated by the Union Pacific's struggle with the Pacific Mail Steamship Line, were particularly severe, and Scott, most upset at the effect on eastern rates, telegraphed Joy, "I agree with you that the destruction of railroad property may be attributed 'to a class of Damn Fools' who refuse to make and maintain rates." Three years later, however, Garrett put Scott in that class after Scott had cut passenger fares; Garrett angrily asked him "must all our tariffs be again thus slaughtered?" Harris came up with an equally bloody metaphor when he told Colfax that "as to 'throat cutting' as applied to Railroads, count me out first, last and always. I object to murder in all forms and especially to suicide."[16]

As railroad leaders readily accepted the analogy of war, they used the language of generals and maintained the same values. Garrett wrote to a vice president in 1877 that, although passenger rates were down, westbound rates had not been "attacked." The year before he had reported that Joseph Hickson of the Grand Trunk "was quite determined on a battle with" the Central. Later, Garrett complained to Scott that "wasteful battles are made against the interests we all represent." From London, Richard Potter, president of the Grand Trunk, offered in September 1876 to mediate the railway dispute then raging. He thought the time propitious because "after months of warfare the relative forces and strength, the powers of offense and defense — the status of each of the combatants can be pretty accurately measured." Officials of the Burlington in Nebraska, locked in a fight with the Union Pacific, refused to compromise with the transcontinental giant, declaring categorically that any concessions "had better be only on the *last* battlefield."[17]

Railway leaders carried their penchant for metaphorical expression into the peace process as well. Henry Fink unintentionally pointed up the practical limitations of the corporate state image in his *Regulation of Railway Rates* published in 1905.

> Rate wars are invariably inconclusive in respect to the controversies that produce them. Some of the competitors may be forced into bankruptcy; but this does not mean victory for the survivors, who cannot obtain war indemnities, nor annex a part of the properties of the vanquished. At the close of the war, the matter at issue remains unsettled and the bankrupt roads can resume the contest with renewed vigor under receiverships, being freed from the obligation of paying interest.

Fink was simply borrowing a decades-old metaphor. Back in 1879 James Clarke, vice president of the Illinois Central, wrote the former president of the road that he thought rumors of consolidation in his region had not "made it necessary up to this moment to even contemplate the terms of surrender. The time has not yet arrived for us to capitulate." A year earlier Adams contended that there was no peace in the East, just extended "periods of truce," during which railway officials increased their strength for "an ever expected renewal of war."[18]

The process through which railway leaders made peace was in perfect harmony with their corporate state image. Negotiations were as structured and complicated as those at any European court. Freight agents and fledgling vice presidents gauged the thinking in rival front offices by talking with their counterparts in various railway capitals. They passed the information they gleaned and their assessment of it on to their vice presidents, who informed their respective presidents if the news seemed that important. If possible, smaller disputes, such as rebates on the St. Louis livestock business, were settled by the railroad agents on the spot. Corporate secretaries of state preferred to focus their attention on important issues involving long-range policy. Only when an unwanted war loomed or when agreed-upon conditions were so bad that a conflict had to be stopped or a new rate structure created did the presidents meet to hammer out the final details of agreements that had been outlined earlier by their vice presidents. These meetings were also highly structured — the chair rotated among the presidents, formal minutes were kept and copies made for all the participants, and each president was allowed to bring his first vice president and other specialists on the topic under discussion. As in international diplomacy, however, the real work appears to have been done in private gatherings held while the formal meetings were adjourned.

Summit meetings were not easily arranged. The paramount consideration was always to enable presidents to save face by not publicly appearing to be bargaining from positions of weakness. A meeting in Philadelphia, for example, was sure to arouse suspicions that Scott had the upper hand in the conflict. A process finally evolved out of twenty years of experience in which the Big Four, as well as officers from other lines, met during the vacation season on neutral ground at Saratoga, New York, or Long Branch, New Jersey. At such spas, railroad presidents could take the waters in public while in private they pursued their diplomatic objectives. Railroadmen everywhere respected the long veranda of the United States Hotel at Saratoga as neutral territory. In other seasons, the Big Four met in New York City. It was centrally located, was not an exclusive capital, was the nation's financial center, and railway executives were frequently there on business. In the 1870s the meetings were always held at the Brevoort House, a neutral gathering place where presidents and vice presidents usually stayed whatever their business when they were in town. The St. Nicholas Hotel had served the same function in earlier decades. With such arrangements railroad presidents could, with straight faces, maintain that they were there for reasons other than those of state.[19]

During the 1870s the agreements forged at these meetings resembled state treaties. They were carefully worded, drawn in technical language even to the point of ending, as one did, with "in witness whereof the persons hereto have executed the same the day and year aforesaid." At the concluding ceremony each president solemnly signed with a flourish under the name of his company. The specialized language and legal form belied the fact that such pacts had no standing before the bar. Henry Fink, whose brother Albert was charged with responsibility for enforcing some arrangements, concluded that treaties would not work because "compliance with the obligations of these agreements depended entirely upon the good faith and enlightened self interest of the contracting parties." In conformity with their image, the "enlightened self interest" of the railway presidents lay primarily with the survival and continued prosperity of their own corporate states. They found it in their interests to obey the laws of trade and commerce and not engage in what Henry Fink called "illegitimate or unhealthy competition," which he defined as competition "conducted without restraint"— an acceptable definition of war.[20]

After studying the problem for over a quarter of a century, Fink finally decided that the laws of competition worked differently for railroads and should somehow be mitigated. Railway presidents had noted this much earlier — they fought the wars. Drawing upon the precedent of the successful Southern Railway and Steamship Association, eastern presidents met in April 1877 to draw up a "memorandum of agreement" in which they attempted to redraw the railway map to eliminate many of the complexities that had long bedeviled balance-of-power considerations in the region. Like their political counterparts, they had to deal with certain distasteful realities, the most important being that the four lines traversed an area with at best only enough traffic for three. Unable to persuade or force one road to liquidate (for as president Henry B. Ledyard of the Michigan Central noted in 1888, a railroad, like a state, "once constructed is built to stay"), their only recourse was to divide the trade as equitably as possible by minimizing competitive differences. Over the next few years these railway leaders agreed on fixed rates that ignored distances, organized pools that allocated tonnage or receipts on some proportion, fixed steamship rates, and created Albert Fink's post as commissioner of the Trunk Line Association to mediate expected disputes. The arrangements were far from perfect, for rebates, drawbacks and other such activities continued unabated. The Association, however, with its provisions rewritten to meet the requirements of the Interstate Commerce Act, remained in existence long after that law was passed.[21]

Ironically, railway leaders' attempts to institutionalize their situation to save their corporate state image forever changed that image. The Trunk Line Association's very existence constituted an important modification of the self-image. Like political leaders of great states, they began to discern that the exercise of their full powers could be self-defeating. The size, influence, and financial resources of such business empires imposed limitations upon their actions. Corporate states, especially those east of Chicago, had matured; except for minor adjustments, their modern territorial configurations were fixed for years to come, their internal structures well established and tested, their normal traffic configurations known. Railroad leaders had much to gain from a stabilized situation in which they could depend upon profitable rates, a known and reliable proportion of the traffic, and profits high enough to keep the stockholders satisfied. They stood to gain little from declaring war on their neighbors. Survival and security became strategic goals in direct proportion to what their companies stood to lose in a war; and those stakes had risen astronomically by the mid-1880s.

AFTERWORD

Railroad leaders by then finally realized that their internal views, and the actions and values they prompted, conflicted with the nation's more self-assured character. Rail executives carried their corporate state image to extremes at the very moment the United States finally healed the wounds of war and ended its Reconstruction travails to enjoy a measure of long-awaited national unity. In their frantic quests for corporate security, railways by the 1880s had alienated many people, even some who depended upon them, such as shippers, farmers, consumers, and local, state, and federal officeholders. Railroad leaders were a decade late in recognizing that the national uncertainty that had helped prompt their corporate state image's creation had radically changed.

The gulf between the rail's self-image and the character of America had become so great by the 1880s that even Robert E. Lee's brilliant artillery chief, E. Porter Alexander, who became a railway official after the conflict, feared for the consequences to his industry and the general public. In an 1887 pamphlet, the ex-Confederate wrote that he was so distressed by the antagonisms that he was willing to support the creation of new constitutional limitations to "protect both the railroads and the people, each from the other."[22] He did not get his amendments, but he did live long enough to see the federal government, prodded by angry voters and the Populist and Progressive movements, extend its regulatory function to all forms of interstate commerce.

The subordination of the railroad leaders' self-image to that of the larger national will forced that distinctive and colorful generation of postwar barons to give way to a less obtrusive set of managers more attuned to the paths of compromise and stability and more in character with the national mood. For the first time railroad leaders were compelled to alter their image to accord with the main elements of the larger national character; they no longer mirrored and helped shape that image. The language used in railway offices everywhere showed that. After sixty years railway officials had to be forced to do what D. Kimball Minor had asked way back in the second number of his *Journal*, namely, give "the people of the United States a unity of feeling, a harmony of interests, and a facility of social intercourse, which must long bind themselves together as one great family."[23] In their odyssey, however, railways left their physical and intellectual marks on America and its character. Most important they eased the manifold fears and doubts that had long eroded the national character. Paradoxically, they imparted such a sense of confidence to the American experiment that the government was emboldened to dominate them.

INTRODUCTION

1. Michael Kammen, *People of Paradox: An Inquiry Concerning the Origins of American Civilization* (New York, 1973); James Oliver Robertson, *American Myth, American Reality* (New York, 1980); Rush Welter, *The Mind of America, 1820–1860* (New York, 1975); David Potter, *People of Plenty: Economic Abundance and the American Character* (Chicago, 1954); John Kenneth Galbraith, *The Affluent Society* (Boston, 1958); Christopher Lasch, *The Culture of Narcissism: American Life in An Age of Diminishing Expectations* (New York, 1979).

2. Kenneth Boulding, *The Image: Knowledge in Life and Society* (Ann Arbor, 1956), passim.

3. Robertson, *American Myth*, 14; Boulding, *The Image*, 54, 6.

4. Bruce Mazlish, *Railroads and the Space Program* (Cambridge, Mass., 1965), 7; Michel Foucault, *The Order of Things: An Archaeology of the Human Sciences* (New York, 1973), xi; Leo Marx, *The Machine in the Garden: Technology and the Pastoral Ideal in America* (New York, 1964), 11; Robertson, *American Myth*, 21.

CHAPTER 1

1. Harold Livesay et al., "Does America Still Exist?" *Harper's Magazine* 268 (March 1984), 52, all citations.

2. *The American Railroad Journal* (hereinafter cited as *ARJ*), Dec. 30, 1837.

3. Bureau of the Census, *Historical Statistics of the United States: Colonial Times to 1957* (Washington, D.C., 1961), 427.

4. Douglas T. Miller, *The Birth of Modern America* (New York, 1970), passim.

5. Pennsylvania, House, "Report of the Committee on Inland Navigation and Internal Improvement, relative to a further improvement of the state by canals and rail-roads," *Journal* II, 1830–31, p. 5.

6. *ARJ*, Jan. 31, 1835; ibid., Aug. 1843 (from March 1843 to Dec. 1844 the *ARJ* was published monthly).

7. Charles M. Caldwell, "Thoughts on the Moral and Other Indirect Influences of Rail-Roads," *The New England Magazine* 2 (Jan.–June 1832), 293.

8. *ARJ*, Dec. 2, 1840; ibid., Aug. 1, 1840; ibid., Jan. 30, 1845.

9. All toasts found in *ARJ*, Oct. 1, 1839.

10. *ARJ*, Jan. 2, 1847; ibid., April 22, 1837.

11. *ARJ*, March 15, 1839; ibid., March 11, 1837; ibid., Oct. 6, 1832.

12. *ARJ*, June 15, 1842; Pennsylvania, House, "Annual Report of the 'Cumberland Valley Rail Road Company' to the Legislature," *Journal* II, 1838–39, p. 153.

13. *ARJ*, July 1843.

14. *ARJ*, Mar. 7, 1835; ibid., Nov. 14, 1835.

15. *Niles' National Register*, Jan. 19, 1839; *ARJ*, Nov. 1844.

16. "Southern Atlantic and Mississippi Railroad," *DeBow's Review* 1 (1846), 23.

17. *ARJ*, Jan. 30, 1847, cited; ibid., May 27, 1847, cited; ibid., March 10, 1849, remainder of citations.

18. *ARJ*, Sept. 18, 1847; ibid., Oct. 7, 1848; ibid., Feb. 1, 1842; ibid., Sept. 1, 1838.

CHAPTER 2

1. *ARJ*, June 28, 1851.

2. *ARJ*, Dec. 17, 1853; *ibid.*, Jan. 18, 1851.

3. *ARJ*, Jan. 18, 1851.

4. Ronald Christ, "Walt Whitman: Image and Credo," *American Quarterly*, 17 (Spring 1965), 103.

5. Eli Bowen, *The Pictorial Sketch-Book of Pennsylvania* (Philadelphia, 1852), 13.

6. *ARJ*, July 25, 1846; ibid., July 9, 1853.

7. Bradford Torrey and Francis Allen (eds.), *The Journal of Henry D. Thoreau* (New York, 1962), V, 266.

8. *ARJ*, July 17, 1847.

9. *ARJ*, July, 1844.
10. "Statistics and Speculations Concerning the Pacific Railroad," *Putnam's Monthly Magazine*, 2 (Sept. 1853), 271.
11. William H. Brown, *The History of the First Locomotives in America* (New York, 1874), 90.
12. Ibid., 144, 145.
13. Quoted in Marx, *Machine in the Garden*, 108.
14. Henry David Thoreau, *Walden: A Writer's Edition* (New York, 1961), 90; Bowen, *Sketch-Book*, 13.
15. B.A. Botkin and Alvin F. Harlow (eds.), *A Treasury of Railroad Folklore* (New York, 1953), 77.
16. Nathaniel Hawthorne, "The Celestial Railroad," *Major Writers of America*, ed. Perry Miller et al. (New York, 1962), 740.
17. Torrey and Allen, *Thoreau*, III, 274.
18. Thoreau, *Walden*, 90–91.
19. Christ, "Whitman: Image," 97.
20. G. Ferris Cronkhite, "The Transcendental Railroad," *The New England Quarterly*, 24 (Sept. 1951), 311; A.L. Plumstead et al. (eds.), *The Journals and Miscellaneous Notebooks of Ralph Waldo Emerson* (Cambridge, Mass., 1975), XI, 374.
21. Cronkhite, "Transcendental Railroad," 315.

CHAPTER 3

1. Charles P. Shiras, "The Railway Car," *Hunt's Merchants' Magazine*, 26 (April 1852), 497.
2. *Niles' Weekly Register*, March 14, 1829.
3. William Jackson, *Lecture on Railroads . . . Before the Massachusetts Charitable Mechanic Association* (Boston, 1829), 19, 20.
4. Pennsylvania, House *Journal*, II, 1830–32, p. 595; Caldwell, "Thoughts," 595.
5. *Niles' Register*, May 21, 1831.
6. Pennsylvania, House, "Resolutions of the Legislature of the State of Louisiana, in relation to a Rail-Road from the Mississippi to the City of Washington," *Journal*, II, 1832–33, p. 43.
7. *ARJ*, Oct. 15, 1836.
8. *ARJ*, Dec. 19, 1835.
9. *ARJ*, Sept. 10, 1836.
10. *ARJ*, Feb. 15, 1842, first citation; ibid., Oct. 17, 1835, not cited; ibid., Dec. 1, 1839, remainder of citations.
11. *ARJ*, June 12, 1845.

12. *ARJ,* March 1843.
13. *ARJ,* July 31, 1845.
14. *ARJ,* Jan. 24, 1846; ibid., April 18, 1846.
15. *ARJ,* April 25, 1846.
16. Ibid.
17. "SA & MR," *DeBow's,* 1, 27, 33.
18. *ARJ,* May 16, 1846.
19. *ARJ,* June 6, 1846.
20. *ARJ,* June 20, 1846.
21. J.E. Thomson to L.P. Grant, May 14, 1846, in the L.P. Grant Papers, Atlanta Historical Society, Atlanta, Box 1, Folder 1; *ARJ,* Feb. 20, 1847.

CHAPTER 4

1. Shiras, "The Railway Car."; *ARJ,* Feb. 11, 1832.
2. *ARJ,* Sept. 1, 1839; *Niles' Weekly Register,* May 21, 1831; Pennsylvania, House *Journal,* II, 1832–33, p. 42.
3. Pennsylvania, House, "Report on Inland Navigation and Internal Improvement," *Journal,* II, 1827–28, p. 670.
4. *ARJ,* Aug. 1843.
5. *Niles' Register,* March 14, 1829; *ARJ,* June 26, 1845.
6. *Niles' Register,* May 21, 1831; Caldwell, "Thoughts," 298.
7. Caldwell, "Thoughts," 298.
8. Merton Sealts (ed.), *Journals and Notebooks of Emerson,* X, 99.
9. *Niles' Register,* July 25, 1835; Pennsylvania, House *Journal* II, 1832–33, p. 670.
10. Pennsylvania, House, "Report Upon the construction of the Sunbury and Erie rail-road," *Journal,* II, 1838–39, pp. 884–35. Ward's italics.
11. *ARJ,* April 28, 1832; ibid., Jan. 14, 1832; ibid., Jan. 9, 1836.
12. Caldwell, "Thoughts," 292.
13. Pennsylvania, House, "Governor Joseph Hiester's Annual Message," *Journal,* 1821–22, p. 16.
14. Caldwell, "Thoughts," 296.
15. "Report of the Board of Directors of Internal Improvements of the State of Massachusetts . . . ," *North American Review* 63 (April 1829), 531.
16. Thomas Earle, *A Treatise on Rail-Roads* (Philadelphia, 1830), 105.
17. Caldwell, "Thoughts," 299.

18. *ARJ*, Dec. 20, 1834; *Proceedings of the Meeting of the Citizens . . . of Philadelphia in relation to the Great Pennsylvania Rail Road. . . .* (Philadelphia, 1846), 13; *ARJ*, April 4, 1848.

CHAPTER 5

1. Shiras, "The Railway Car."
2. E.H. Derby, *Two Months Abroad . . . By a Rail-Road Director of Massachusetts* (Boston, 1844), 50, 51.
3. *ARJ*, Oct. 16, 1845.
4. *ARJ*, Feb. 2, 1832; ibid., Nov. 4, 1844; Proceedings of sundry Citizens of Baltimore, . . ." *North American Review* 56 (Jan. 1827), 65.
5. Caldwell, "Thoughts," 297.
6. Ibid.; *Niles' Weekly Register*, Aug. 29, 1835.
7. Caldwell, "Thoughts," 297.
8. *Niles' Register*, March 3, 1832; Caldwell, "Thoughts," 297.
9. *ARJ*, July 1, 1838; ibid., June 3, , 1848
10. *ARJ*, Jan. 9, 1836; ibid., Jan. 15, 1840.
11. *Niles' Register*, July 25, 1835.
12. *ARJ*, April 1843.
13. *ARJ*, July 13, 1850.
14. *ARJ*, Dec. 1844.
15. *ARJ*, Jan. 16, 1845.
16. *ARJ*, July 3, 1845; ibid., Sept. 15, 1841.
17. *ARJ*, Feb. 15, 1842; ibid., Sept. 19, 1846.
18. *ARJ*, Oct. 30, 1845.

CHAPTER 6

1. Pennsylvania, House *Journal*, 1822–23, p. 15; U.S. Congress, House, DeWitt Clinton to Lt. Col. John J. Abert, Jan. 26, 1832, Doc. 133, 22d Cong., 1st Sess., 5; Pennsylvania, House, "Governor J. Andrew Shulze's Annual Message," *Journal*, II, 1826–27, p. 6.
2. Pennsylvania, House, "Report of the Commissioners for promoting the internal improvement of the state," *Journal*, II, 1824–25, p. 266.
3. "1829 Report of Massachusetts Directors," *North American Review* 63 (April 1829), 532.
4. Jackson, *Lecture*, 25, 26.
5. *ARJ*, Aug. 24, 1833; ibid., Sept. 15, 1841; ibid., March 17, 1849.

6. Pennsylvania, House *Journal*, II, 1830–31, p. 597.

7. *Brief View of the System of Internal Improvement of the State of Pennsylvania.* . . . (Philadelphia, 1831), 32 cited, 33–34 circular theory; Walter Christaller, *Central Places in Southern Germany,* trans. Carlisle Baskin (Englewood Cliffs, New Jersey, 1966).

8. *ARJ,* July 14, 1849; ibid., Sept. 8, 1849.

9. Jackson, *Lecture,* 26.

10. *Niles' Register,* March 26, 1831; *ARJ,* Jan. 18, 1834; Richmond article reprinted in *Niles' Register,* March 26, 1831.

11. *Proceedings of 1846 Meeting for Pennsylvania Railroad,* 13.

12. *ARJ,* Aug. 24, 1833.

13. *ARJ,* Sept. 1844.

14. *ARJ,* July 10, 1847; ibid., June 17, 1848; John Stover, *American Railroads* (Chicago, 1961), 88–90.

15. *Correspondence between the Lehigh Coal and Navigation Company and the Beaver Meadow Rail Road and Coal Company* (n.p., 1835), 5; *ARJ,* Sept. 15, 1841; *ARJ,* Oct. 20, 1849; *ARJ,* Oct. 13, 1849.

CHAPTER 7

1. Brown, *First Locomotives,* 219; Charles Glaab, *Kansas City and the Railroads: Community Policy in the Growth of a Regional Metropolis* (Madison, Wisc., 1962), 31; *Eighth Annual Report of the Board of Managers of the Sunbury and Erie Rail Road Company* (Philadelphia, 1859), 15; *ARJ,* June 15, 1842.

2. *ARJ,* Feb. 28, 1835; ibid., Nov. 14, 1835; ibid., Oct. 8, 1853; *North Pennsylvania Railroad to Connect Philadelphia with North Pennsylvania, Western New York, The Lakes and Canada* (Philadelphia, 1853), 24.

3. *ARJ,* Aug. 7, 1852; ibid., April 9, 1853.

4. *Report of the President and Managers of the Danville and Pottsville Rail Road* (Philadelphia, 1839), 21; Pennsylvania, House, "Report of the Majority of the Committee on Internal Improvements relative to Granting the Baltimore and Ohio Railroad Company the right of way through Pennsylvania," *Journal,* II, 1845, p. 595; *ARJ,* Feb. 27, 1847; *ARJ,* Oct. 6, 1849.

5. *ARJ,* Aug. 14, 1845; ibid., Sept. 11, 1845; Bowen, *Sketch-Book,* 188, 189.

6. "Proceedings of 1827 Meeting of sundry Citizens of Balti-

more," *North American Review,* 68; *ARJ,* Dec. 1, 1840; *ARJ,* Sept. 27, 1851.

7. "Col. Gadsden's Report," *DeBow's Review* 1, 1846, p. 28.

8. "Proceedings of 1827 Meeting of sundry Citizens of Baltimore," *North American Review,* 62.

9. *ARJ,* Sept. 19, 1835; ibid., Nov. 14, 1835; ibid., Sept. 27, 1851; ibid., Oct. 8, 1853.

10. *Debates in the General Assembly of the State of New Jersey on the South Jersey Central and Air Line Railroad Bill* (Trenton, 1854), 9.

11. "SA & MR," *DeBow's* 1, 27; *Fifth Annual Report of the Directors of the Pennsylvania Railroad Company* (Philadelphia, 1852), 17.

12. *ARJ,* Nov. 25, 1837.

13. *ARJ,* May 29, 1847; ibid., June 15, 1850.

14. *Niles' Register,* March 14, 1835.

15. "Proceedings of 1827 Meeting of sundry Citizens of Baltimore," *North American Review,* 72.

16. *ARJ,* July 6, 1850; ibid., Nov. 20, 1847; Pennsylvania, House, "Report of the majority of the committee, appointed to examine the route of the Gettysburg rail road," *Journal,* II, 1837–38, p. 481.

17. Anon., "The Pacific Railroad and How It is to be Built," *Putnam's Monthly Magazine* 2 (Nov. 1853), 500, 501, 507.

CHAPTER 8

1. *ARJ,* Dec. 16, 1848; Michael Aaron Rockland, trans., *Sarmiento's Travels in the United States in 1847* (Princeton, 1970), 133.

2. *ARJ,* May 23, 1846; Carl Condit, *The Port of New York: A History of the Rail and Terminal System from the Grand Central Electrification to the Present* (Chicago, 1982), 94. See also Leo Marx, "Closely Watched Trains," *The New York Review of Books,* March 15, 1984.

3. Ian R. Bartky, "The Invention of Railroad Time," *Railroad History,* no. 148 (Spring 1983), 13–22; B.A. Botkin and Alvin F. Harlow, eds., *A Treasury of Railroad Folklore* (Chicago, 1953), 514–15.

4. Pennsylvania, House *Journal,* 1822–23, p. 15; U.S. Congress, House, *Railroad-Portage Summit, Ohio to Hudson River,* 22nd Cong., 1 sess., doc. no. 133 (1832), p. 5; Earle, *A Treatise on Rail-Roads,* 104–106.

5. "Proceedings of 1827 Meeting of sundry Citizens of Baltimore," *North American Review*, 71.

6. *Niles' Weekly Register*, May 23, 1829.

7. Ibid., April 23, 1831; *ARJ*, Nov. 15, 1834; Brown, *First Locomotive*, 145.

8. See Bruce Mazlish (ed.), *The Railroad and the Space Program: An Exploration in Historical Analogy* (Cambridge, Mass., 1965); *Niles' Weekly Register*, June 27, 1835.

9. *Niles' Register*, April 25, 1835; ibid., Dec. 9, 1848.

10. Ibid., April 25, 1835; *ARJ*, Sept. 15, 1841.

11. *ARJ*, Jan. 14, 1832; *Niles' Register*, April 23, 1831.

12. Caldwell, "Thoughts," 294–95.

13. *ARJ*, Oct. 17, 1835; ibid., Jan. 1, 1842, Nov. 1844.

14. *First Report of the Board of Directors of the Steubenville & Indiana Railroad Company* (Steubenville, 1850), 14.

15. David S. Landes, *Revolution in Time: Clocks and the Making of the Modern World* (Cambridge, Mass., 1983), 314.

CHAPTER 9

1. *Niles' Weekly Register*, June 25, 1831; Athens *Southern Banner*, April 17, 1845; *ARJ*, March 20, 1847; *Niles' Register*, May 28, 1835.

2. Pennsylvania, House, "Report of commissioners for promoting the internal improvements of the state," *Journal*, II, 1825–26, p. 267.

3. Bowen, *Sketch-Book*, 19, 20.

4. Botkin, *Railroad Folklore*, 68, 69.

5. Pennsylvania, House, "1837 Governor's annual message to Legislature," *Journal*, II, 1837–38, p. 24.

6. Pennsylvania, House *Journal*, II, 1825–26, p. 267.

7. George Rogers Taylor, *The Transportation Revolution, 1815–1860* (New York, 1968), 79.

8. Botkin, *Railroad Folklore*, 67, 68.

9. Pennsylvania, House *Journal*, II, 1830–31, p. 597; *Report of the Committee on Inland Navigation and Internal Improvement* (Harrisburg, 1834), 7.

10. Review of *Chemins de Fer Americains*, by Guillaume-Tell Poussin, *North American Review* 95 (April 1837), 435.

11. *ARJ*, July 1, 1839.

12. S.J. Packer, *Extract Relative to the Importance of the Lehigh Navigation, to the Commonwealth* (Harrisburg, 1835), 7.

13. Pennsylvania, House, "Report of the committee on inland navigation and internal improvement, relative to the Baltimore and Susquehanna rail road company," *Journal*, II, 1828–29, p. 542.

14. Joseph C.G. Kennedy, *Preliminary Report of the Eighth Census, 1860* (Washington, 1862), 237.

15. Lorenzo Sherwood, "Agencies to be Depended on in the construction of internal improvements, with Reference to Texas . . . ," *DeBow's Review* 19 (1855), 203–205.

16. Louis Hartz, *Economic Policy and Democratic Thought: Pennsylvania 1776–1860* (Cambridge, Mass., 1948), 52–53.

17. Pennsylvania, House, "Governor David Porter's annual message to the Legislature, *Journal*, II, 1840, p. 34; *ARJ*, May 13, 1848.

CHAPTER 10

1. *ARJ*, March 27, 1852.

2. J.D.B. DeBow, *Statistical View of the United States . . . Being A Compendium of the Seventh Census* (Washington, 1854), 189; John F. Stover, *Iron Road to the West* (New York, 1978), 215.

3. *ARJ*, Jan. 10, 1852; Daniel Calhoun, *The American Civil Engineer: Origins and Conflict* (Cambridge, 1960), 50–53; Herman Haupt, *General Theory of Bridge Construction* (New York, 1951); Herman Haupt, "On the Resistance of The Vertical Plates of Tubular Bridges," *Journal of the Franklin Institute*, Ser. 3, XXVI (Oct. 1853); *ARJ*, Oct. 8, 1853; *ARJ*, Aug. 28, 1852.

4. *ARJ*, Oct. 22, 1853.

5. Pennsylvania, House *Journal*, II, 1845, p. 599; Susan Smith and Harrison Heyford (eds.), *The Journals of Emerson* XIV, 29.

6. *ARJ*, Feb. 28, 1852.

CHAPTER 11

1. *The Weekly Baltimore Patriot*, May 24, 1851, in the Robert Swann Collection, Maryland Historical Society, Baltimore, Box #3.

2. *ARJ*, April 17, 1845.

3. *ARJ*, April 1844.

4. *ARJ*, Jan. 30, 1845.

5. *ARJ*, Dec. 29, 1849.

6. *Address of Committee of Seven to the Citizens of Philadelphia* (Philadelphia, 1846), 5.

7. *First Annual Report of the Directors of the Pennsylvania Rail-Road* (Philadelphia, 1847), 10.

8. *Fifth Pennsylvania Railroad Annual Report*, 82.

9. *ARJ*, May 14, 1853; *Fourth Annual Report of the Directors of the Pennsylvania Rail-Road* (Philadelphia, 1851), 31.

10. *ARJ*, Oct. 8, 1853; ibid., Dec. 13, 1851.

11. *ARJ*, July 14, 1849; ibid., Jan. 20, 1849.

12. *ARJ*, Oct. 6, 1849; ibid., Oct. 13, 1849.

13. *ARJ*, Dec. 1, 1842; ibid., April 10, 1847.

14. *ARJ*, June 26, 1852; ibid., July 2, 1853; ibid., July 16, 1853; ibid., Oct. 8, 1852.

15. *ARJ*, Nov. 13, 1852.

16. *ARJ*, April 23, 1853.

17. Herman Haupt to J.E. Thomson, June 2, 1852, Herman Haupt Letterbook, Historical Society of Pennsylvania, Philadelphia, p. 56, *ARJ*, Aug. 28, 1852, italics added.

18. Haupt to Thomson, May 17, 1852, Haupt Letterbook, p. 38; *ARJ*, Nov. 20, 1852.

19. *ARJ*, Jan. 22, 1853; *Twelfth Annual Report of the Directors of the Pennsylvania Railroad* (Philadelphia, 1859), 19.

20. Thomson to John Work Garrett, Feb. 19, 1859, B&O Papers, Maryland Historical Society, Baltimore; Garrett to Charles Moran, March 11, 1859, ibid.

21. Thomson to Garrett, June 2, 1859, ibid.; Samuel Barlow to Garrett, June 4, 1859, ibid.; Thomson to Garrett, July 1, 1859, ibid.; Garrett to Thomson, July 2, 1859, ibid.; Thomson to Garrett, July 6, 1859, ibid.

22. Garrett to Thomson, July 11, 1859, ibid.; Barlow to Garrett, July 26, 1859, ibid.

23. Thomas C. Cochran, "The Legend of the Robber Barons," *The Pennsylvania Magazine of History and Biography* 74 (July 1950), 307–321.

CHAPTER 12

1. Robert Sobel, *The Entrepreneurs; Explorations Within the American Business Tradition* (New York, 1974), 113.

2. Alfred D. Chandler, Jr., *The Railroads: The Nation's First Big Business* (New York, 1965), 9.

3. Charles Elliott Perkins to John Murray Forbes, Feb. 18, 1884, in Thomas C. Cochran, *Railroad Leaders, 1845–1890: The Business Mind in Action* (Cambridge, Mass., 1953), 436.

4. James Hurst, *The Legitimacy of the Business Corporation in*

the Law of the United States, 1780–1970 (Charlottesville, 1970), 1–12; Alfred D. Chandler, Jr., "The Railroads: Pioneers in Modern Corporate Management," *Business History Review* 39 (Spring 1975), 16–40.

5. Alfred Chandler and Stephen Salsbury, "The Railroads: Innovators in Modern Business Administration," in Mazlish (ed.), *The Railroad and Space Program*, 158–59; Perkins, "Memorandum of Organization," 1875, in *Railroad Leaders*, 430; M.L. Sykes to A. Keep, Dec. 17, 1883, in Julius Grodinsky, *The Iowa Pool: A Study in Railroad Competition, 1870–1884* (Chicago, 1950), 159.

6. Forbes to Peter Geddes, Sept. 1, 1885, in *Railroad Leaders*, 340; Perkins to Robert Harris, April 7, 1871, ibid., 429; Grodinsky, *Iowa Pool*, 154.

7. Maury Klein, "The Strategy of Southern Railroads," *The American Historical Review*, 73 (April 1968), 1067; Anna J. Reynolds, "The John Edgar Thomson School . . . ," (unpublished mss., Thomson Foundation, Philadelphia), 2; James Joy to John C. Green, July 13, 1869, in *Railroad Leaders*, 368.

8. Julius Grodinsky, *Transcontinental Railway Strategy, 1869–1893* (Philadelphia, 1962), 13.

9. John King to Garrett, July 12, 1875, B&O Papers; Garrett to King, July 28, 1878, ibid.; Scott to Garrett, April 2, 1877, ibid.; reported in Sykes to Joy, Aug. 3, 1870, in *Iowa Pool*, 16; Joy to John Newell, March 27, 1871, in *Railroad Leaders*, 368; Forbes to David Dows, March 15, 1877, in *Railroad Leaders*, 335; King to Garrett, March 20, 1875, B&O Papers.

10. M.H. Smith to Garrett, April 17, 1879, B&O Papers; George B. Roberts to Garrett, April 21, 1879, ibid.

11. King to J.N. Camden, Nov. 5, 1877, B&O Papers; William K. Ackerman to L.V.F. Rudolph, Oct. 17, 1878, in *Railroad Leaders*, 240; Garrett to Scott, May 24, 1877, B&O Papers; Charles F. Adams, *Railroads: Their Origins and Problems* (New York, 1878), 194.

12. King to Garrett, Feb. 2, 1875, B&O Papers; Minutes of the Board of Directors of the Pennsylvania Railroad, May 28, 1879 (formerly in the Office of the Secretary of the Penn Central Railroad, Philadelphia); Brooks to Thomas Doane, Aug. 14, 1872, in *Railroad Leaders*, 338; Kimball to Everett Gray, Feb. 25, 1885, in *Railroad Leaders*, 373.

13. King to Garrett, Jan. 12, 1874, B&O Papers; King to Garrett, June 19, 1874, ibid.

14. Perkins to J.M. Walker, Nov. 11, 1875, in *Iowa Pool*, 95; Col-

lis P. Huntington to Charles Colton, Oct. 23, 1876 in *Ellen Colton vs. Leland Stanford et al*, in Superior Court of State of California in and for the County of Sonoma, 1882, III, 1739; Ackerman to Randolph, Nov. 23, 1881, in *Railroad Leaders*, 244; Ackerman to Amos Hopkins, Nov. 27, 1882, in *Railroad Leaders*, 245; John H. Devereux to Horace Clark, Sept. 19, 1871, in *Railroad Leaders*, 313; Robert Harris to Schuyler Colfax, March 13, 1877, in *Railroad Leaders*, 350.

15. Ackerman to Randolph, Nov. 22, 1881,in *Railroad Leaders*, 244; Frederick Billings to Villard, March 14, 1881, in James B. Hedges, *Henry Villard and the Railways of the Northwest* (New York, 1930), 85; J.F. Barnard to Joy, April 12, 1873, in *Iowa Pool*, 35; Sykes to A. Keep, Oct. 16, 1875, in *Iowa Pool*, 96; Edgar T. McLees? to Garrett, Aug. 24, 1877, B&O Papers.

16. Ackerman to Randolph, Nov. 22, 1881, in *Railroad Leaders*, 244; John Griswold to Perkins, Jan. 8, 1884, ibid.; Address of Herman Haupt to Convention of Southern Railroad and Steamship Lines, Sept. 25, 1885, *The Railway World*, 630; PRR Board Minutes, May 28, 1879; Henry Fink, *Regulation of Railway Rates on Interstate Freight Traffic* (New York, 1905), 12; Joy to William P. Burrall, Jan. 26, 1854, in *Railroad Leaders*, 365; Scott to Joy, April 25, 1874, in *Iowa Pool*, 42; Garrett to Scott, June 2, 1877, B&O Papers; Harris to Colfax, March 13, 1877, in *Railroad Leaders*, 350.

17. Garrett to King, June 6, 1877, B&O Papers; Garrett to Scott, Sept. 9, 1876, ibid.; Garrett to Scott, May 24, 1877, ibid.; Richard Potter to Garrett, Sept. 4, 1876, ibid.; G. Tyson to Perkins, April 23, 1877, in *Iowa Pool*, 81.

18. Henry Fink, *Railway Rates*, 11; James C. Clarke to William Osborn, Dec. 20, 1879, in *Railroad Leaders*, 294; Adams, *Railroads*, 191.

19. Summary of peace procedures from B&O Correspondence 1873–1881.

20. Memorandum of Agreement made this 8th day of June 1877, B&O Papers; Fink, *Railway Rates*, 15, 10.

21. Ledyard to James Clements, Nov. 21, 1880, in *Railroad Leaders*, 404; Fink, *Railway Rates*, 27.

22. E. Porter Alexander, *Railway Practice: Its Principles and Suggested Reforms Reviewed* (New York, 1887), 44.

23. *ARJ*, Jan. 7, 1832.

BIBLIOGRAPHY

MANUSCRIPT COLLECTIONS AND NEWSPAPERS

American Railroad Journal, 1832–1858.

Athens (Ga.) *Southern Banner*, 1834–1847.

Baltimore & Ohio Railroad Papers. Maryland Historical Society, Baltimore.

Barlow, Samuel. Papers. Huntington Library, San Marino, Calif.

Bell, James Martin. Papers. Duke Univ. Library, Durham, N.C.

Black, Nellie Peters. Collection. Univ. of Georgia Libraries, Athens.

Carnegie, Andrew. Papers. Library of Congress, Washington, D.C.

DeBow's Review, 1846–1860.

Georgia Railroad and Banking Company. Minutes of Stockholder Meetings, Office of the Georgia Railroad Bank and Trust Company, Augusta.

————. Minutes of the Board of Directors. Office of the Georgia Railroad Bank and Trust Company, Augusta.

Grant, Lemuel P. Papers. Atlanta Historical Society, Atlanta.

Haupt, Herman. Papers, 1824–1905. Yale Univ. Library, New Haven.

Jackson (Mississippi) *Flag of the Union*, 1850–1854.

Niles' Weekly Register, 1829–37; *Niles' National Register*, Sept. 1837–1849.

Palmer, William Jackson. Papers. Colorado State Historical Society, Denver.

Philadelphia Evening Bulletin, 1857–60.

Swan, Robert. Papers. Maryland Historical Society, Baltimore.

Tennessee *Register*, Feb. 22, 1982.

Wall, Joseph. Collection of Carnegie Papers. Grinnell College, Grinnell, Iowa.

BOOKS, ARTICLES, PAMPHLETS, REPORTS,
REVIEWS, AND GOVERNMENT DOCUMENTS

Address of John W. Garrett to the Board of Directors of the Baltimore & Ohio Railroad Company, Upon His Re-Election as President of that Company, December 1865. Baltimore: Printing Office, 1865.

Address of the Committee of Seven to the Citizens of Philadelphia and of Pennsylvania, Appointed at a Town Meeting, Held at Philadelphia, on the 28th of April 1846. Philadelphia: Jasper Harding, 1846.

Alexander, E. Porter. *Railway Practice: Its Principles and Suggested Reforms Reviewed.* New York: Putnam's, 1887.

Alvarez, Eugene. *Travel on Southern Antebellum Railroads, 1828–1860.* University: Univ. of Alabama Press, 1974.

Ames, Charles E. *Pioneering the Union Pacific: A Reappraisal of the Builders of the Railroad.* New York: Appleton-Century Crofts, 1969.

Annual Reports of the Directors of the Pennsylvania Railroad Company, 1847–1882.

Anon. *Brief View of the System of Internal Improvement of the State of Pennsylvania. . . .* Philadelphia: Lydia R. Bailey, 1831.

Anon. "Jack Lantern's Railroad Speculations." *Putnam's Monthly Magazine* 2 (July 1853).

Anon. *Report of the delegates to the Warren Convention. Published by Order of the Philadelphia Board of Trade.* Philadelphia: John Thompson, 1833.

Anon. review of Poussin, Guillaume. *Chemins de Fer Amercains; Historique de leur Construction; Prix de Revient et Produit; Mode d'Administration adopte; Résumé de la Législation qui les régit.* Paris: n.p., 1836, in *North American Review* 95 (April 1837).

Anon. review of *Proceedings of sundry Citizens of Baltimore, convened for the Purpose of Devising the most efficient Means of Improving the Intercourse between that City and the Western States.* Baltimore: William Wooddy, 1827, in *North American Review* 56 (Jan. 1827).

Anon. review of *Report of the Board of Directors of Internal Improvements of the State of Massachusetts on the Practicability and Expediency of a Rail Road from Boston to the Hudson River, and from Boston to Providence, submitted to the General Court,*

January 16, 1829. . . . N.p., n.d., in *North American Review* 63 (April 1829).

Anon. review of *Report of the Engineers on the Reconnaissance and Surveys made in reference to the Baltimore and Ohio Rail Road.* Baltimore: William Wooddy, n.d., and *Second Annual Report of the President and Directors* to the Stockholders of the Baltimore and Ohio Rail Road Company. Baltimore: William Wooddy, n.d., in *North American Review* 62 LXII (Jan. 1829).

Anon. "Statistics and Speculations Concerning the Pacific Railroad." *Putnam's Monthly Magazine* 20 (Sept. 1853).

Anon. "The Pacific Railroad and How it is to be Built." *Putnam's Monthly Magazine* 2 (Nov. 1853).

Autobiography of Andrew Carnegie. Boston: Houghton Mifflin, 1920.

Barrow, Craig. Review of *Lewis Carroll: A Celebration,* by Edward Guiliana (New York: Clarkson Potter, 1981). Chattanooga *Times,* May 8, 1982.

Barton, Roger. "The Camden and Amboy Railroad Monopoly." *Proceedings of the New Jersey Historical Society* 12 (1927).

Bishop, Avard L. "The State Works of Pennsylvania." *Transactions of the Connecticut Academy of Arts and Sciences* 13 (Nov. 1907).

Black, J.S. *Railroad Monopoly. Argument . . . to the Judiciary Committee of the Senate of Pennsylvania, Thursday, May 24, 1883.* N.p.: n.p., n.d.

Black, Nellie Peters, ed. *Richard Peters: His Ancestors and Descendants.* Atlanta: Foote & Davies Co., 1904.

Bode, Carl., ed. *Collected Poems of Henry Thoreau.* Chicago: Packard & Co., 1943.

Botkin, B.A., and Alvin F. Harlow. *A Treasury of Railroad Folklore. The Stories, Tall Tales, Traditions, Ballads, and Songs of the American Railroad Man.* New York: Crown, 1953.

Boulding, Kenneth. *The Image: Knowledge in Life and Society.* Ann Arbor: The Univ. of Michigan Press, 1961.

Bowen, Eli. *The Pictorial Sketch-Book of Pennsylvania. Its Scenery, Internal Improvements, Resources, and Agriculture, Popularly Described.* Philadelphia: Willis P. Hazard, 1852.

Brown, William H. *The History of the First Locomotives in America: From Original Documents and the Testimony of Living Witnesses.* Rev. ed. New York: D. Appleton, 1874.

Burgess, George H., and Miles C. Kennedy. *Centennial History of the Pennsylvania Railroad Company, 1846–1946.* Philadelphia Pennsylvania Railroad Co., 1949.

Caldwell, Charles. "Thoughts on the Moral and Other Indirect Influences of Rail-Roads." *The New England Magazine* 2 (Jan.–June, 1832).

Calhoun, Daniel. *The American Civil Engineer: Origins and Conflict.* Cambridge: Harvard Univ. Press, 1960.

Carson, Robert. *Main Line to Oblivion: The Disintegration of New York Railroads in the Twentieth Century.* Port Washington, N.Y.: Kennekat Press, 1971.

Chandler, Alfred D., Jr. *The Railroads: The Nation's First Big Business.* New York: Harcourt, Brace & World, 1965.

––––––. *The Visible Hand: The Managerial Revolution in American Business.* Cambridge: Belknap Press, 1977.

Christ, Ronald. "Walt Whitman: Image and Credo." *American Quarterly* 17 (Spring, 1975).

Christaller, Walter. *Central Places in Southern Germany.* Translated by Carlisle Baskin. Englewood Cliffs, N.J.: Prentice-Hall, 1966.

Clark, Thomas D. "The Montgomery and West Point Railroad Company." *Georgia Historical Quarterly* 17 (March 1933).

Cochran, Thomas. "The Legend of the Robber Barons." *The Pennsylvania Magazine of History And Biography* 74 (July 1950).

––––––. *Railroad Leaders, 1845–1890: The Business Mind in Action.* Cambridge: Harvard Univ. Press, 1953.

Cohen, Henry. *Business and Politics in America from the Age of Jackson to the Civil War: The Career Biography of W. W. Corcoran.* Westport, Conn.: Greenwood, 1971.

Cohen, Norm. *Long Steel Rail: The Railroad in American Folksong.* Urbana: Univ. of Illinois Press, 1981.

Condit, Carl W. *The Port of New York; A History of the Rail and Terminal System from the Grand Central Electrification to the Present.* Chicago: Univ. of Chicago Press, 1981.

Correspondence Between the Lehigh Coal and Navigation Company, and the Beaver Meadow Rail Road and Coal Company, relative to the Interference of the Location of the Rail Road, with the future extension of the Lehigh Navigation. N.p.: n.p., 1835.

Cronkhite, G. Ferris. "Walt Whitman and the Locomotive." *American Quarterly* 6 (Summer 1954).

––––––. "The Transcendental Railroad." *The New England Quarterly* 24 (Sept. 1951).

Daughen, Joseph and Peter Binzen. *The Wreck of the Penn Central.* New York: Signet, 1971.

Davis, Patricia. *End of the Line: Alexander J. Cassatt and the Pennsylvania Railroad.* New York: Neale Watson Academic Publications, 1978.

Debates in the General Assembly of the State of New Jersey, on the South Jersey Central and Air Line Railroad Bill, and the Extension of the Charter of the Camden and Amboy Railroad Company. . . . Trenton, N.J.: State Gazette Office, 1854.

DeBow, J.D.B. *Statistical View of the United States, A Compendium of the Seventh Census.* Washington, D.C.: Beverley Tucker, 1854.

Derby, E.H. *Two Months Abroad: or, a Trip to England, France, Baden, Prussia, and Belgium in August and September, 1843. By A Rail-Road Director of Massachusetts.* Boston: Redding & Co., 1844.

Earle, Thomas. *A Treatise on Rail-Roads and Internal Communications. Compiled from the Best and Latest Authorities with Original Suggestions and Remarks.* Philadelphia: Mifflin & Parry, Printers, 1830.

Eighth Annual Report of the Board of Managers of the Sunbury and Erie Rail Road Company, to the Meeting of the Stockholders, Held February 14, 1859. Philadelphia: Crissy & Markley, 1859.

Eleventh Annual Report of the President and Directors to the Stockholders of the Baltimore and Ohio Rail Road Company. Baltimore: Lucas & Deaver, 1837.

Emerson, Ralph Waldo. *Conduct of Life* (1860). In *The Selected Writings of Ralph Waldo Emerson,* edited by Brooks Atkinson. New York: The Modern Library, 1950.

First Report of the Board of Directors, of the Steubenville & Indiana Rail Road Company, Accompanied by A Map of the Route and Connecting Lines. Steubenville: Steubenville Daily, 1850.

Fourth, Sixth, and Eleventh Annual Reports of the Catawissa Rail Road Company. . . . Philadelphia: H.G. Leisenring's, 1864, 1866, 1871.

Glaab, Charles N. *Kansas City and the Railroads: Community Policy in the Growth of a Regional Metropolis.* Madison: Univ. of Wisconsin Press, 1962.

Goodrich, Carter. *Government Promotion of American Canals and Railroads, 1800–1890.* New York: Columbia Univ. Press, 1960.

Gray, Francine Du Plessix. *Lovers and Tyrants.* New York: Simon and Schuster, 1976.

Grodinsky, Julius. *Jay Gould: His Business Career, 1867–1892.* Philadelphia: Univ. of Pennsylvania Press, 1957.

————. *The Iowa Pool: A Study in Railroad Competition, 1870–1884.* Chicago: Univ. of Chicago Press, 1950.

————. *Transcontinental Railway Strategy, 1869–1893: A Study of Businessmen.* Philadelphia: Univ. of Pennsylvania Press, 1962.

Gutman, Herbert G. "Trouble on the Railroads in 1873–1874: Prelude to the 1877 Crisis?" *Labor History* 2 (Spring 1971).

Harrison, Eliza Cope. *Philadelphia Merchant: The Diary of Thomas P. Cope, 1800–1851.* South Bend, Ind.: Gateway Editions, 1978.

Hartz, Louis. *Economic Policy and Democratic Thought: Pennsylvania 1776–1860.* Chicago: Quadrangle, 1968.

Hawthorne, Nathaniel. "The Celestial Railroad." In *Major Writers of America,* edited by Perry Miller et al. New York: Harcourt, Brace & World, 1962, pp. 738–46.

Heath, Milton S. *Constructive Liberalism: The Role of the State in Economic Development in Georgia to 1860.* Cambridge: Harvard Univ. Press, 1954.

————. "Public Railroad Construction and the Development of Private Enterprise in the South Before 1861." *The Journal of Economic History,* Supplement 10 (1950).

Ingle H.L., and James A. Ward. *American History.* Boston: Little, Brown, 1978.

Jackson, William. *Lecture on Rail Roads Delivered January 12, 1829, Before the Massachusetts Charitable Mechanic Association.* Boston: Croker & Brewister, 1829.

Jones, Charles Edwin. "The Railroad to Heaven." *North Dakota Quarterly* 40 (Autumn 1972).

Kammen, Michael. *People of Paradox: An Inquiry Concerning the Origins of American Civilization.* New York: Knopf, 1973.

Kirkland, Edward Chase. *Dream and Thought in the Business Community, 1860–1900.* Chicago: Quadrangle, 1964.

Klein, Maury. "In Search of Jay Gould." *Business History Review* 52 (Summer 1978).

Kneass, Samuel H. *Report of the Survey of a Line of Rail Road from the Borough of Marietta to Intersect the Columbia & Philadelphia Rail Road, near the Little Conestoga.* Lancaster: John Reynolds, Printer, 1832.

Kolko, Gabriel. *The Triumph of Conservatism: A Reinterpretation of American History.* New York: The Free Press, 1963.

Larson, Henrietta. *Jay Cooke: Private Banker.* Cambridge: Harvard University Press, 1936.

Larson, John L. *Bonds of Enterprise: John Murray Forbes and Western Development in America's Railway Age.* Cambridge: Harvard Univ. Press, 1984.

Licht, Walter. *Working for the Railroad: The Organization of Work in the Nineteenth Century.* Princeton, N.J.: Princeton Univ. Press, 1983.

Lee, Ivy L. *The Railroads and Human Nature. Address . . . at Thirty-Fifth Semi Annual Dinner. The American Railway Guild, May 19, 1914.* N.p.: n.p., n.d.

MacGill, Caroline F. *History of Transportation in the United States Before 1860.* Washington, D.C.: Carnegie Institution of Washington, 1917.

Martin, Albro. *Enterprise Denied: Origins of the Decline of American Railroads, 1897–1917.* New York: Columbia Univ. Press, 1971.

———. "The Troubled Subject of Railroad Regulation in the Gilded Age — a Reappraisal." *Journal of American History* 61 (1974).

Marx, Leo. *The Machine in the Garden: Technology and the Pastoral Ideal in America.* New York: Oxford Univ. Press, 1964.

Mazlish, Bruce. *The Railroad and the Space Program.* Cambridge: Harvard Univ. Press, 1965.

Miller, ?. *Report of the Committee on Inland Navigation and Internal Improvement.* Harrisburg, Pa.: Henry Welsh, 1834.

Miller, Douglas T. *The Birth of Modern America, 1820–1850.* New York: Pegasus, 1970.

Miller, Edward. *First Report of Edward Miller, Engineer in Chief of the Sunbury and Erie Rail Road to the Managers, January 12, 1839.* Philadelphia: John C. Clark, 1839.

Morison, Elting. *From Know-How to Nowhere.* New York: Basic Books, 1974.

Nevins, Allan. *Study in Power: John D. Rockefeller, Industrialist and Philanthropist.* New York: Charles Scribner's Sons, 1953.

"New Yorker." *To the Governor and the People of Pennsylvania.* N.p.: n.p., 1861.

North, Douglas C. *The Economic Growth of the United States, 1790–1860.* Englewood Cliffs, N.J.: Prentice-Hall, 1961.

Nugent, Walter T.K. *The Money Question During Reconstruction.* New York: W.W. Norton, 1967.

Organization of the United Companies under the name of the Philadelphia, Wilmington and Baltimore Rail Road Company with

the Articles of Union and Second Annual Report of the President and Directors. . . . Philadelphia: John C. Clark, 1838.
Overbey, Daniel L. *Railroads: The Free Enterprise Alternative.* New York: Quorum Books, 1982.
Overton, Richard C. *Perkins/Budd: Railway Statesmen of the Burlington.* Westport, Conn.: Greenwood Press, 1982.
Packer, S.J. *Extract Relative to the Importance of the Lehigh Navigation, to the Commonwealth, from the Report of the Committee of the Senate of Pennsylvania, upon the subject of the Coal Trade.* Harrisburg: Hugh Hamilton & Son, 1835.
Pennsylvania Canal Commission, Reports and Documents, RG-17, W2C-20. Pennsylvania Historical and Museum Commission, Harrisburg.
Pennsylvania *Journal of the House of Representatives.* Harrisburg: Various publishers, 1818–1855.
Pennsylvania Railroad. *Annual Reports of the Directors to the Stockholders, nos.* 1–30. Philadelphia: 1847–1877.
Pennsylvania Railroad. Minutes of the Board of Directors. Office of the Secretary of the Penn Central Railroad, Philadelphia.
Pennsylvania *Senate Journal.* Harrisburg: Various publishers, 1818–1855.
Philadelphia and Columbia Railroad. Superintendent's Report, for the Fiscal Year ending November 30, 1853. N.p.: n.p., n.d.
Philadelphia's Great North Route. North Pennsylvania Railroad, to Connect Philadelphia with North Pennsylvania, Western New York, the Lakes and Canada West. Philadelphia: Brown's Steam Power Printing, 1853.
Phillips, Ulrich B. *A History of Transportation in the Eastern Cotton Belt to 1860.* New York: Columbia Univ. Press, 1908.
Plumstead, A.W. et al., eds. *The Journals and Miscellaneous Notebooks of Ralph Waldo Emerson.* Vols. VII–XIV. Cambridge: Harvard Univ. Press, 1969–1978.
Poor, Henry V. *History of the Railroads and Canals of the United States of America.* New York: J.H. Schultz, 1860.
———. *Manual of Railroads of the United States 1869–1870.* New York: H.V. and H.W. Poor, 1869.
Poor, H.V. and H.W., *Poor's Manual, 1889.* New York: H.V. and H.W. Poor, 1889.
Proceedings of the Meeting of the Citizens of the City and County of Philadelphia in Relation to The Great Pennsylvania Rail Road from Philadelphia via Harrisburg to Pittsburgh, with the Ad-

dress of the Committee to the People of Pennsylvania. Philadelphia: Steam Press, 1846.

Proceedings of the Rail-Road Convention, Assembled at Harrisburg, March 6, 1838. Philadelphia: Peter Hay, 1838.

Railways in New Brunswick. Tracts Issued By the Council of the Railway League. Saint John, N.B.: J. & A. McMillan, 1849.

Report of the Chief Engineer of the Danville and Pottsville Rail Road Company. With A Report of the President and Managers to the Stockholders. January 1833. Philadelphia: I. Ashmead & Co., 1833.

Report of the Directors of the Michigan Central Railroad Company to the Stockholders . . . June 1853. Boston: Eastburn's Press, 1853.

Report of the President and Directors of the Harrisburg, Portsmouth, Mount Joy, & Lancaster Rail Road Company, to the Stockholders, September 7, 1855. Philadelphia: John C. Clark & Son, 1855.

Report of the President and Managers of the Allegheny Valley Rail Road to the Stockholders with the Chief Engineer's Report, and Treasurer's Statement. Read February 7, 1854. Pittsburgh: W.S. Haven, 1854.

Report of the President and Managers of the Danville and Pottsville Rail Road Company, to the Stockholders, January 1839. Philadelphia: Joseph & William Kite, 1839.

Report of the Superintendent of the Danville & Pottsville Rail Road. Philadelphia: Printed for the Company, 1838.

Review of an Address of the Joint Board of Directors of the Delaware and Raritan Canal and Camden and Amboy Railroad Companies to the People of New Jersey. By a Citizen of Burlington. Philadelphia: C. Sherman, 1848.

Riegal, Robert E. *The Story of the Western Railroads from 1852 through the Reign of the Giants.* Lincoln: Univ. of Nebraska Press, 1926.

Ringwalt, J.L. *Development of Transportation Systems in the United States.* Philadelphia: Published by Author, 1888.

Robertson, James Oliver. *American Myth, American Reality.* New York: Hill & Wang, 1980.

Rockland, Michael Aaron, trans. *Sarmiento's Travels in the United States in 1847.* Princeton, N.J.: Princeton Univ. Press, 1970.

Rosenberger, Homer T. *The Philadelphia and Erie Railroad: Its Place in American Economic History.* Potomac, Md.: Fox Hills Press, 1975.

Rubin, James. "Canal or Railroad? Imitation and Innovation in the

Response to the Erie Canal in Philadelphia, Baltimore, and Boston." *Transactions of the American Philosophical Society* 51, Pt. 7 (Nov. 1961).

Russell, Robert R. "The Pacific Issue in Politics Prior to the Civil War." *Mississippi Valley Historical Review* 12 (Sept. 1925).

Saunders, Richard. *The Railroad Mergers and the Coming of Conrail.* Westport Conn.: Greenwood Press, 1978.

Schotter, H.W. *The Growth and Development of the Pennsylvania Railroad Company.* Philadelphia: Allen, Lane & Scott, 1927.

Second, Fourth Annual Reports of the Board of Directors of the North Pennsylvania Railroad Company. . . . January 8, 1855. Philadelphia: Crissy & Markley, 1855, 1857.

Second Annual Report of the Directors and Chief Engineer of the Cleveland & Mahoning R.R. Co., December 20, 1854. Cleveland: Harris, Fairbank & Co., 1855.

Second Annual Report of the President and Directors of the Huntingdon and Broad Top Mountain Rail Road and Coal Company. Philadelphia: J.B. Chandler, 1855.

Second Report of the Directors of the New York and Erie Railroad Company to the Stockholders, February 3, 1841. New York: Egbert Hedge, 1841.

Shariati, Ali. *Civilization and Modernization.* Houston: Free Islamic Literatures, 1978.

Sixth Annual Report of the Board of Directors of the Pittsburgh, Fort Wayne and Chicago Railway Company to the Stock and Bondholders for the year Ending December 31, 1867. Pittsburgh: Barr & Myers, 1868.

Snow, C.P. *Last Things.* New York: Charles Scribner's Sons, 1970.

Sobel, Robert. *The Entrepreneurs: Explorations within the American Business Tradition.* New York: Weybright and Talley, 1974.

Stayer, Samuel N. "James Martin Bell: Ironmaster and Financier, 1799–1870." Ph.D. diss., Duke Univ., 1970.

Stilgoe, John R. *Metropolitan Corridor: Railroads and the American Scene.* New Haven: Yale Univ. Press, 1983.

Stover, John F. *American Railroads.* Chicago: Univ. of Chicago Press, 1961.

———. *Iron Road to the West: American Railroads in the 1850s.* New York: Columbia Univ. Press, 1978.

———. *The Railroads of the South, 1867–1900: A Study in Finance and Control.* Chapel Hill: Univ. of North Carolina Press, 1955.

Taylor, George Rogers. *The Transportation Revolution, 1815–1860.* New York: Harper & Row, 1951.

——, and Irene B. Neu. *The American Railroad Network, 1861–1890.* Cambridge: Harvard Univ. Press, 1956.

Temin, Peter. *The Jacksonian Economy.* New York: W.W. Norton & Co., 1969.

Thomson, J. Edgar. *Before Railroads: A Contemporary View of the Agriculture, Industry, and Commerce of the South in the Forties.* Nashville, Tenn.: n.p., 1928 (?).

Thoreau, Henry David. *Walden: A Writer's Edition.* New York: Holt, Rinehart & Winston, 1961.

Torrey, Bradford, and Francis H. Allen, eds. *The Journal of Henry D. Thoreau.* New York: Dover Publications, 1962.

Trautwine, John C. *Extracts from the report on the Survey of the Lackawanna and Lanesboro' Railroad. . . .* Philadelphia: T.K. & P.G. Collins, 1856.

Travelers Official Railway Guide of the United States and Canada, June 1868. Reprint. Ann Arbor, Mich.: National Railway Publication Co., 1968.

Trumble Alfred. *The Fast Men of America: Or, Racing with Time from Cradle to Grave. The Romance and Reality of Life on the Railroad.* New York: R.K. Fox, 1882.

Tuchman, Barbara W. *A Distant Mirror: The Calamitous Fourteenth Century.* New York: Knopf, 1978.

——. *Practicing History: Selected Essays* New York: Knopf, 1981.

U.S. Congress, House. *Abstract of the Returns of the Fifth Census.* 22nd Cong., 1st sess., 1830, Doc. No. 269.

U.S. Congress, House. *Affairs of the Union Pacific Company.* 42nd Cong., 3d sess., 1873. Rept. 78.

U.S. Congress, House. *Railroad-Portage Summit, Ohio to Hudson River; Letter from DeWitt Clinton.* Doc. 133. 22nd Cong., 1st sess., February 29, 1832.

U.S. Congress, House. *The Disposal of Subsidies Granted Certain Railroad Companies.* 44th Cong., 1st sess., 1876, Misc. Doc. 176, pt. 1.

Wall, Joseph. *Andrew Carnegie.* New York: Oxford Univ. Press, 1970.

War of the Rebellion: A Complation of the Official Records of the Union and Confederate Armies. 128 vols. Washington: U.S. Government Printing Office, 1880–1901.

Ward, James A. "A New Look at Antebellum Southern Railroad Development." *The Journal of Southern History* 39 (Aug. 1973).

————. *J. Edgar Thomson: Master of the Pennsylvania*. Westport: Greenwood Press, 1980.

————. *That Man Haupt: A Biography of Herman Haupt*. Baton Rouge: Louisiana State Univ. Press, 1973.

Watkins, J. Elfreth. *History of the Pennsylvania Railroad Company 1846–1896*. Philadelphia: N.p., 1896.

Weber, Thomas. *The Northern Railroads in the Civil War, 1861–1865*. New York: King's Crown Press, Columbia Univ. Press, 1952.

Welter, Rush. *The Mind of America, 1820–1860*. New York: Columbia Univ. Press, 1975.

White, John H. *The American Railroad Passenger Car*. Baltimore: The Johns Hopkins Press, 1978.

Wiebe, Robert H. *The Search for Order, 1877–1920*. New York: Hill and Wang, 1967.

Willard, Daniel. *The Railroads and the Public: An Address . . . to the Students of Dartmouth College, Hanover, N.H., March 22, 1915*. N.p.: n.p., n.d.

Wilson, William B. *History of the Pennsylvania Railroad Company: With Plan of Organization, Portraits of Officials, and Biographical Sketches*. Philadelphia: Henry T. Coates & Co., 1899.

Wood, W.K. "The Georgia Railroad and Banking Company." *Georgia Historical Quarterly* 57 (Winter 1973).

Woodward, C. Vann. *Reunion and Reaction: The Compromise of 1877 and the End of Reconstruction*. Garden City, N.J.: Doubleday, 1956.

├─┼─┼─┼─┼─┼─┼─┼─┼─┼─┼─┼─┼─┼─┤

Railroads (*cont.*)
ments of commerce, 140; and intelligence, 59, 60; and knowledge, 56, 58, 59; and ladies, 71;
and land grants, 82; and land
values, 81, 83, 84, 85, 87, 89; legal control of, 133; and liberty
and equality, 58; metaphor for
hopes, 11; and milk, 65; and
money, 114; as moral influences,
60, 61, 62, 63, 71, 73; and national character, 57, 134; and national harmony, 58; and national
power, 49; and nation's interest,
57, 139; in new intellectual
world, 57; and patriotic duty, 16;
and peace, 149; pools, 147; and
private aggrandizement, 142; and
poor, 75, 77, 78; population, 88;
as private enterprise, 126; and
prosperity, 16, 81, 149; and public's business, 142; rates, 156; and
the rich, 73; self image, 128; self
serving, 129; and social change,
80; and social structure, 69, 71,
76, 81; and speculations, 145; and
summit meetings, 167; survival
and security, 169; and time, 77,
107, 114, 115; treaties, 167; unity,
61, 149, 150; and urban competition, 133; and urban poor, 62;
and wealth, 53, 63; and weapons,
43; and the West, 94, 95
Real estate values, 88
Richmond *Enquirer*, 88
Roberts, George B., 160
Robertson, James O., 3, 5, 6
Rock Island R.R., 156, 161, 162
Roebling, John, 26, 53, 97
Roosevelt, Theodore R., 127

Sarmiento, Domingo F., 106
Savannah *Georgian*, 22, 78, 85, 96
Scientific American, 111
Scott, Thomas A., 154, 159, 161, 165
Sherwood, Lorenzo, 125
Slidell, John, 50
Sobel, Robert, 151
South Carolina Canal and Railroad
Company, 34

South Carolina R.R., 88
South Jersey Central and Air Line
R.R., 100
Southern Atlantic and Mississippi
R.R., 24, 51
Southern Pacific, 162
Southern Railroad of Mississippi, 52
Speculators, 146
Springfield (Ill.) *Journal*, 87
Springfield (Mass.) *Gazette*, 33
Standard Oil, 160
Steubenville and Indiana R.R., 114
Stewart, Andrew, 50
St. Louis *New Era*, 53
Stock Speculation, 143, 144
Sunbury and Erie R.R., 61, 96, 98
Sykes, M.L., 156

Texas and Pacific R.R., 162
Thomson, John E., 53, 146, 147, 148,
149, 154, 157
Thoreau, Henry D., 31, 33, 36, 37, 38;
and *Walden*, 36, 37
Through traffic, 157
Time: and American democracy, 107;
and discipline, 107; and distance,
109, 111, 112; measurement, 107;
as money, 110, 112; and poor, 114;
and profits, 112, 114; "railroad
time," 107; and space, 111, 112;
and speed, 109; standardization,
108; time machine, 115
Tracey, John F., 159
Transcontinental R.R., 48, 49, 51, 96,
104-5, 143, 150
Trenton (Tenn.) *Emporium*, 25, 101
Trunk Line Association, 168
Trunk lines, 153
Turner, Frederick J., 4
Turnpikes, 118, 119
Twain, Mark, 137

Union, 112
Union Pacific, 159, 163, 165
United States Navy, 44
Unity, 13, 106, 115
Urban wars, 15

Van Buren, Martin, 102
Vanderbilt, William H., 154, 159

Railroads and the Character of America, 1820–1887 has been composed on a Compugraphic digital phototypesetter in ten point Caledonia with two points of spacing between the lines. Caledonia Bold and Italic were selected for display. The book was designed by Frank O. Williams, typeset by Metricomp, Inc., printed offset by Thomson-Shore, Inc., and bound by John H. Dekker & Sons. The paper on which the book is printed carries acid-free characteristics for an effective life of at least three hundred years.

THE UNIVERSITY OF TENNESSEE PRESS : KNOXVILLE